THE DOCTOR WHO QUIZ BOOK

By the same author

THE SECOND DOCTOR WHO QUIZ BOOK
THE DOCTOR WHO CROSSWORD BOOK

THE DOCTOR WHO QUIZ BOOK

Compiled by
Nigel Robinson

TARGET

A TARGET BOOK

published by
the Paperback Division of
W. H. ALLEN & Co. PLC

A Target Book
Published in 1981
By the Paperback Division of
W.H. Allen & Co. PLC
44 Hill Street, London W1X 8LB

Reprinted 1982
Reprinted 1984

Typeset by V & M Graphics Ltd, Aylesbury, Bucks
and printed in Great Britain by
Hunt Barnard Printing Ltd, Aylesbury, Bucks.

ISBN 0 426 20143 4

CONTENTS

AUTHOR'S ACKNOWLEDGMENTS

I would like to thank John Nathan-Turner, the BBC *Doctor Who* Office and especially Ian Levine for their invaluable assistance in the compiling of this book.

N.R.

FOREWORD

How many times did the second Doctor yell, 'When I say run, run!'? What quantity of jelly babies did the fourth Doctor consume? How often did the third Doctor say, 'Reverse the polarity of the neutron flow', and why does the fifth Doctor wear celery in his frock-coat lapel? These are just four of the questions and answers that do *not* appear in this book! Nevertheless, I strongly recommend this fascinating volume which, as the Producer of *Doctor Who*, I shall find a useful addition to the reference section of the office library.

Having watched *Doctor Who* on and off since it began, and having been closely connected with the programme for five years – I didn't realise how much I'd forgotten! A joy to peruse.

John Nathan-Turner
Producer
Doctor Who

THE QUESTIONS

1. What does the word TARDIS mean?
2. Why did the Doctor steal a TARDIS and leave Gallifrey?
3. Our sun and its solar system lie in the Milky Way galaxy. By what other name is this galaxy known?
4. What unusual physical property is shared by the Visians, whom the first Doctor met, and the Spiridons, encountered by the third Doctor?
5. Romana achieved a triple first at the Academy on Gallifrey. What grade did the Doctor receive?
6. Which alien race tried twice to conquer Earth, but later reformed and became peaceful members of the Galactic Federation?
7. In which adventure did the Doctor first use his sonic screwdriver?
8. What is a CVE?
9. Silicon-based life forms are very rare in the Galaxy. Name the two which the Doctor has encountered.
10. On which planet were the Daleks created?
11. For countless centuries the Sontarans have waged a bitter war against which other species?
12. The very first episode of *Doctor Who*, broadcast in 1963, was called *An Unearthly Child*. Who was the Unearthly Child?
13. Whose trademark is to murder people by shrinking them?
14. In which adventure were the Doctor and his companions chased by clockwork soldiers?
15. Which planet has the co-ordinates, from galactic zero centre, of ten, zero, eleven, zero zero by zero two?

1. Who chased the Doctor and his companions through time and space in their own time machine?
2. Ian and Barbara were teachers at Susan's school on Earth. Which one taught science and which one taught history?
3. What was the cause of the 'plague' which was sweeping the planet of the Sensorites when the Doctor visited it?
4. Who were the rulers of Vortis before the coming of the Animus?
5. When the Doctor landed on the planet of the Elders and the Savages, he discovered that his arrival had been anticipated for some time. By what name was he known to Jano's people?
6. The five Keys of Marinus were scattered in different locations throughout the planet. Give the locations of two of the five Keys.
7. In the adventure *Edge of Destruction*, why was the TARDIS rushing backwards in time to the dawn of time itself and to certain destruction?
8. What was the Steel Sky?
9. Who embarked on a 'Mission to the Unknown'?
10. Odysseus ordered the Doctor to present him with a plan to take the city of Troy. The Doctor eventually came up with the idea of the Trojan Horse. What was his first suggestion?
11. What powerful force attracted the TARDIS to the planet Vortis?
12. How did the Doctor immobilise the Meddling Monk's TARDIS in 1066?
13. Who was the 'guardian' of Vicki and Bennett on the planet on which they were stranded?
14. When the TARDIS jumped a time track, what terrible vision of the future did the Doctor and his companions see?
15. What was WOTAN?
16. With which family did Steven and Dodo play a deadly game of Musical Chairs?

17. Who was Maaga?
18. What was the final destination of the Space Ark, on which the Doctor, Steven and Dodo landed?
19. Bret Vyon was a member of the Space Security Service. Who killed him, and why?
20. Name the Aztec lady to whom the Doctor was briefly engaged when the TARDIS materialised in 15th-century Mexico.

1. Only two of the Doctor's companions entered the TARDIS for the first time with the sole intention of making an emergency phone call. Name one of them.
2. What is Romana's full name?
3. Which of the Doctor's companions was attacked by a giant rat in the sewers of London?
4. After the Master had murdered her father, how did Nyssa journey to Logopolis to join the Doctor and Adric?
5. Which of his companions did the Doctor meet at Culloden in 1746?
6. Which of the Doctor's companions married a Welsh Nobel Prize winner and accompanied him on a journey down the Amazon?
7. For which magazine did Sarah Jane Smith do most of her writing?
8. In the adventure *Planet of the Daleks*, who offered Jo Grant the opportunity to start a new life on which alien planet?
9. Which school on Earth did Susan, the Doctor's granddaughter, attend?
10. Which of the Doctor's companions was an extremely competent astro-physicist, but when the Doctor met her was working as a librarian?
11. On which planet did the Doctor and his companions meet Steven?
12. Who did Victoria stay with when she finally left the Doctor?
13. Which of the Doctor's companions was a sailor who had been assigned a six-months' shore posting when he met the Time Lord?
14. When she regenerated, Romana took on the likeness of which alien princess?
15. Which of the Doctor's companions chose to stay behind with the fleeing Trojans after the destruction of their city, and changed her name to Cressida?

1. Who were the Faceless Ones?
2. How was the weather of Earth controlled from the Moon in the year 2070?
3. Name the helicopter pilot who saved the lives of the Doctor and his friends when the TARDIS landed on an Australian beach.
4. How did the Doctor destroy the Seeds of Death?
5. Who was the old friend whom the Doctor unexpectedly met in Tibet and who had been taken over by the Great Intelligence?
6. Immediately after the Doctor's first regeneration, which of his companions most suspected that he was not really the Doctor?
7. Who was Salamander?
8. The War Lord captured soldiers from many different periods in Earth's history and made them refight their wars. What was his ultimate intention in doing this?
9. On which planet did the Doctor hide Milo Clancey?
10. How many Daleks did the Doctor initially 'humanise'?
11. What was the ultimate objective of the Weed Creature in *Fury from the Deep*?
12. Who was Varga?
13. In the adventure *The Web of Fear*, where in the London Underground did the TARDIS materialise?
14. When the Doctor and Jamie materialised in the *Silver Carrier*, the rocket orbiting the Wheel in Space, how did the TARDIS warn its passengers of the dangers outside?
15. What circumstances brought about England's second ice age?
16. Who was the Controller of the Wheel in Space?
17. When the TARDIS materialised in the Land of Fiction, how did the intelligence controlling that land attempt to lure Jamie and Zoe out of the TARDIS?
18. Who was the mute who aided Jamie in his search for Victoria in the 19th century?

19. Why did the Krotons order that the Gonds should periodically send their two best scholars into the Dynotrope?
20. Who travelled in space/time capsules called SIDRATs?

1. The Daleks are the mutated survivors of which race?
2. Who is the supreme ruler of all Daleks?
3. Name the evil genius who created the first Daleks.
4. Skaro is a radiation-soaked world of mutant flora and fauna and petrified forests. What caused this devastation?
5. In their quest for galactic supremacy, the Daleks attempted to start a war between Earth and which other planet?
6. How did Theodore Maxtible and Edward Waterfield accidentally bring the Daleks to the 19th century?
7. The Daleks used which other alien race as 'guard dogs'?
8. Who was the Guardian of the Solar System who betrayed it to the Daleks in the 41st century?
9. On the planet Mechanus, the Daleks fought a duel to the death with which robots?
10. The planet Exxilon is abundant in parrinium, one of the rarest minerals in the Galaxy. Why did (a) the Earth expedition led by Commander Stewart, and (b) the Daleks, come to Exxilon to mine the mineral?
11. How did the first Doctor and his companions learn of the Daleks' plan to pursue them through time and space?
12. Why were the Daleks planning to explode a second neutron bomb when the first Doctor visited Skaro?
13. Why were the Daleks present in great numbers on the planet Kembel in the year 4000?
14. How did the Thals escape the mutation which affected the Daleks?
15. Who was the scientist on the Earth colony of Vulcan who found three Daleks in a Mercury swamp and brought them back to life?
16. How did the second Doctor provoke a vicious civil war between the Daleks on Skaro?
17. Why did the Daleks first invade Earth in the latter half of the 22nd century?
18. Why did the Daleks 'exterminate' their creator in his bunker on Skaro?

19. Before their first invasion of Earth in the mid 22nd century, how did the Daleks weaken the Earthmen's resistance?
20. Why was the Doctor so reluctant to destroy the Daleks when the Time Lords sent him to Skaro to do so?

1. After he had stood trial and the Time Lords had passed sentence on him, where did the Doctor's TARDIS land?
2. Who is the 'mightiest of all the beasts of Peladon'?
3. What lurked in the disused mines beneath the Welsh village of Llanfairfach?
4. Any spaceship landing on Exxilon suffered an immediate power drain. Even the TARDIS was not immune. What was the cause of these power losses?
5. Why were the Silurians and the Sea Devils forced to retreat to their underground hibernation chambers?
6. How are the Autons armed?
7. In the year 2540 the Earth Government set up a penal colony for political prisoners in which the Doctor was briefly imprisoned. Where was this penal colony?
8. Who were the two Lurman entertainers who brought the Miniscope to Inter Minor?
9. The Daemons first came to Earth over 100,000 years ago with the intention of helping mankind to evolve. Why then did Azal decide to destroy Earth?
10. Who succeeded to the throne of Peladon after the death of King Peladon?
11. Why did the Ambassadors of Death 'kidnap' three astronauts from Earth and arrive on Earth in their spaceship?
12. Which arch enemy of the Doctor seduced Queen Galleia of Atlantis and became King of that land?
13. When Jo announced to the Doctor that she was to be married, what did he give her as a wedding present? Why did she later return it?
14. What was the name of the Doctor's yellow roadster?
15. When the Time Lords returned to him his freedom, to which planet did the Doctor promise to take Jo? Where did they first materialise?
16. What was the Keller Process?
17. When the Doctor began experimenting with his grounded TARDIS, he managed to throw himself into an alternative time/space continuum. How did he power the TARDIS in this experiment?

18. Name the three guerillas who travelled 200 years back in time to kill Sir Reginald Styles.
19. Which High Priest of Peladon and advisor to the King joined forces with Arcturus in an attempt to prevent Peladon from becoming a member of the Galactic Federation?
20. The Doctor and Sarah Jane saw the destruction of one of the 700 Wonders of the Universe. Which one?

1. The first menace of the Doctor's fourth incarnation was Professor Kettlewell's Giant Robot. How did the Doctor destroy it?
2. Who were the 'Three Who Rule'?
3. How did the Logopolitans preserve the Universe beyond its point of natural heat-death?
4. Who was the leader of the Zygons stranded on Earth?
5. Which common Earth substance proved an effective defence against the Fendahleen?
6. The robots on board the Sandminer were divided into three classes. What were they?
7. Which High Priestess of the Sisterhood of the Flame sacrificed herself so that the Doctor might live?
8. What was the City of Death?
9. The Doctor, Leela and K9 met a crew of Minyans who were nearing the end of a 100,000-year quest for the *P7E*. What was the *P7E* and why were the Minyans searching for it?
10. What was the Zygma Experiment?
11. Who was the head of the Company on Pluto?
12. Tremas was the father of Nyssa. How did he die?
13. Which of the Doctor's old foes actually dared to invade Gallifrey?
14. Which King of Kastria did Eldrad plan to usurp?
15. On which planet was the Leisure Hive to be found?
16. When Styre landed on Earth, he found the planet to be uninhabited. Why did he lure the Galsec astronauts down to the planet's surface?
17. How did part of Mandragora reach Earth in the late 15th century?
18. The Creature from the Pit was in reality Erato, the Tythonian Ambassador. Why did Adrasta imprison him in the pit?
19. Whose was the 'Face of Evil'?
20. What is the most dangerous addictive drug in the Universe? And on which planet did Tryst find it?

1. To which caveman did Ian give the secret of fire?
2. Name the King of England whom the first Doctor and his friends met in 12th-century Palestine.
3. Which Duke of the Italian province of San Martino helped the Doctor and Sarah in their fight against the Mandragora Helix?
4. How did the the third Doctor defend the castle of Edward of Wessex and Lady Eleanor from the might of Irongron's men?
5. The first Doctor was the exact double of which Catholic abbot of 16th-century France?
6. Name the English lieutenant who captured the Doctor and his companions at Culloden in 1746.
7. What was the prophecy Cassandra made concerning the fate of Troy, and how did she misinterpret this prophecy?
8. Why did Marco Polo wish to give Kublai Khan the TARDIS as a gift?
9. When the TARDIS crew landed in 15th-century Mexico, why was Barbara mistaken for the reincarnation of the High Priest Yetaxa?
10. Who was the leader of the Saracens when the TARDIS landed in Palestine?
11. When the TARDIS materialised in revolution-torn France, Ian was entrusted with delivering a message to one James Stirling. Who was Stirling?
12. Name the pirate captain who had the first Doctor kidnapped.
13. When the first Doctor had a toothache, to which dentist did he go for treatment?
14. Anne Chaplette was a Protestant serving-girl who made friends with Steven in 16th-century Paris. The Doctor was unable to save her from the St Bartholomew's Day Massacre because even he dared not alter history. But how was it suggested that Anne might have survived the Massacre?
15. Several aliens have landed on Earth before the beginning of the 20th century with the intention of changing history, for good or evil. Name two of them.

1. What are Robomen?
2. In the adventure in Galaxy Four, the Rills calculated that the planet on which they were stranded would be destroyed in fourteen days' time. How long to doomsday did the planet really have?
3. Who challenged the Doctor to the Trilogic Game?
4. What is a Varga plant?
5. Name the four creatures native to Vortis at the time of the visit of the Doctor and his companions.
6. The Mechonoids were robots designed by Earthmen and sent to Mechanus to prepare the planet for colonisation. Some fifty years later, the Mechonoids were still awaiting the colonisers. Why?
7. Who was the secretary of Professor Brett, the inventor of WOTAN?
8. When the Meddling Monk visited England in the 11th century, what form did his TARDIS take?
9. What gift was the Doctor presented with by Tor, leader of the Xerons?
10. On which planet did the Doctor visit an island in the middle of a sea of acid?
11. Why did the scientist Forester murder Farrow, the representative of the Board of Agriculture, in *Planet of Giants*?
12. When the TARDIS crew landed on a 28th-century spaceship, they found that the Sensorites had put the spaceship's crew in a death-like trance. Why had the Sensorites done this?
13. What is a Slyther?
14. Who did Achilles believe the Doctor to be when they met?
15. What name did Vicki give to the Rills' robotic servants?
16. When the first Doctor and his companions returned to the Space Ark seven hundred years after their first visit, how had the relationship between the Humans and the Monoids changed? Who was responsible for this?
17. Why did Bennett kill all the crew of his spaceship except Vicki?

18. Name the captain of the spaceship which had been in orbit around the planet of the Sensorites when the TARDIS landed there.
19. Why were the Doctor, Ian, Vicki, Barbara and Steven imprisoned by the Mechonoids?
20. Who was the leader of the Voords when the TARDIS landed on Marinus?

1. How were the first Cybermen created?
2. Name the two planets of the Cybermen.
3. Tobias Vaughn hoped to use the power of the Cybermen to conquer the world. How did he then hope to destroy them?
4. What is a Cybermat?
5. What was the planet of gold, and what important role did it play in the great Cyberwar?
6. On which planet was the tomb of the Cybermen to be found?
7. What did the Cybermen intend to do with the personnel of the Snowcap Ice Base at the South Pole after the destruction of Earth?
8. How did the Cybermen on the Moon hope to destroy Earth in the year 2070?
9. In *The Invasion*, how did the Cybermen propose to retaliate after the first Cybertransport fleet was destroyed by atomic warheads?
10. How was this plan thwarted?
11. Why did the Cybermen return to Earth's solar system after their defeat in the Cyberwar?
12. Who was the American general in charge of the Snowcap Ice Base in the Antarctic who was killed by the Cybermen?
13. How was the planet Mondas destroyed?
14. Why was the International Electromatic Corporation so essential to the Cybermen's take-over of Humans in their invasion attempt in the late 20th century?
15. How do Cybermats locate their intended victims?
16. Why were the Doctor and Lester and Stevenson of the Nerva crew so necessary to the Cybermen's plans when the Cybermen returned to Earth's solar system after the Cyberwar?
17. The Cybermen made their first television appearance in *The Tenth Planet*. What was the name of the Tenth Planet?
18. Name the two Cybermen who led the attacks on the Snowcap Ice Base.

19. Where was the main Cyberfleet stationed, awaiting instructions to join their fellow Cybermen in the invasion of Earth which had been engineered by Tobias Vaughn?

20. The Cybermen devised a complicated plan to lure Humans from the Wheel in Space to the *Silver Carrier*, the rocket in orbit around the Wheel. What was the plan?

1. Why was the Doctor finally forced to reveal his position in time and space to the Time Lords?
2. How did he do this?
3. What was Edward Waterfield's dying request to the Doctor?
4. Who was the Goddess of Atlantis to whom the Doctor and his companions were very nearly sacrificed?
5. Whom did the 'Master' of the Land of Fiction serve?
6. When the TARDIS materialised in space on the dark side of the Moon, who fired a missile at the Doctor and his companions?
7. Who were the robotic servants of the Dominators?
8. Why was the TARDIS stolen from Gatwick airport in 1966?
9. Who was Arturo Villar?
10. How did the Doctor destroy the Ice Warriors who threatened Earth during the second ice age?
11. What was the Krotons' Dynotrope in reality?
12. What were the functions of the Wheel in Space?
13. Who was Milo Clancey's former partner, who was presumed to be dead?
14. Name the King of Atlantis during the second Doctor's visit to that place.
15. When the Doctor arrived on the Earth colony of Vulcan, for whom was he mistaken?
16. Who was the head of the Issigri Mining Company, who was in league with the Space Pirates?
17. When he first visited the monastery of Det-sen in the 17th century, why was the Doctor entrusted with the safe keeping of the holy ghanta?
18. How did Salamander meet his death?
19. The Great Intelligence promised Padmasambhava long life and great knowledge in return for his help in an experiment. What was this experiment, and how was Padmasambhava deceived?
20. How did the Doctor defeat the Macra?

1. Which Human aided the Cybermen in their invasion of Earth in the late 20th century?
2. What grave threat to the world did the insecticide DN6 pose?
3. Why did the Mandragora Helix wish to conquer Earth?
4. How did the Silurians intend to alter the climate of Earth, so making it a more comfortable place for them to inhabit?
5. What did the Axons give as their reason for coming to Earth? What was their true purpose?
6. Scaroth travelled 400 million years back in time to prevent the explosion of his spaceship. Why did the Doctor follow him to ensure that the explosion did take place?
7. What was the first stage of the first Nestene invasion of Earth?
8. The Zygons encountered by the Doctor in Scotland had crash-landed there centuries before. Why did they eventually decide to take over and colonise Earth?
9. Who was the Military Commander of the Kraals who intended to lead the invasion fleet to Earth?
10. Name the millionaire botanist who had a Krynoid pod brought to England and was nearly responsible for the destruction of the entire Human race.
11. Which Human was used by the Spiders of Metebelis Three in their quest for domination on Earth?
12. Why did the Ice Warriors of Mars wish to invade Earth?
13. How did the Kraals plan to wipe out Earth's population prior to their colonising the planet?
14. What was the purpose of Operation Golden Age?
15. Name the government minister in charge of Operation Golden Age and the scientist who aided him.
16. How did the Nestenes use the Autons and the Replicas to prepare for their first invasion of Earth?
17. What dangers to the world did the Doctor see in Professor Eric Stahlmann's Inferno Project?

18. Which city was the first to be attacked by the War Machines in accordance with WOTAN's plan for world domination?
19. The Giant Robot planned to wipe out the Human race because it was corrupt. What did it then intend to do?
20. How did the Doctor and Liz Shaw finally defeat the Nestene Consciousness and the Autons?

1. Who was the Time Monster?
2. Name all the members of the Assessment Committee who came to Peladon to investigate the planet's application to join the Galactic Federation.
3. Which alien race was known by the sobriquet of 'Dragons'?
4. After the Master's attempt to destroy Axos failed, how did the Doctor defeat the space parasite?
5. What was the power source of Professor Thascales' TOMTIT machine?
6. Who was the young archer from the Middle Ages who befriended the Doctor and Sarah, and killed Linx the Sontaran?
7. What was the consequence for the Solonians of Professor Jaeger's experiments on the atmosphere of their planet?
8. Why were the inhabitants of Inter Minor wary of aliens to the point of xenophobia?
9. Omega, insane with hatred for his fellow Time Lords, swore revenge on Gallifrey. How did he take his revenge?
10. Who destroyed the Doomsday Machine and, in so doing, willingly gave up his own life?
11. Which alien race developed space travel and journeyed to other worlds, including Earth (where they landed in Peru), but when the Doctor met them had become a superstitious and backward people?
12. What were the two dominant powers of the Milky Way in the 26th century?
13. Who was BOSS?
14. Name the white witch who helped the Doctor and UNIT in their battle with Azal and the Master.
15. Where did the Doctor discover the underground hibernation chambers of the Silurians?
16. What was the Mind of Evil?
17. When the Doctor and Sarah Jane arrived back in London from the Middle Ages, why were they arrested by the military?

18. When the Doctor first met her, Sarah Jane Smith was impersonating Lavinia Smith. Who was Lavinia Smith?
19. Name the home planet of the Daemons.
20. In *The Terror of the Autons*, the Nestene Consciousness was brought to Earth by means of a radio telescope. How did the Doctor and the Master succeed in sending it back into space?

1. How were the Daleks defeated when the first Doctor met them on Skaro?
2. Who was the Master of the Fifth Galaxy who helped the Daleks in their Master Plan?
3. How did the Daleks lose their war with the Venusian Colonies in the space year 17,000?
4. How did Davros help the Thals destroy the Kaled City on Skaro?
5. Why did he do this?
6. Name the young resistance fighter who accompanied Barbara to the Dalek mines when the Daleks invaded Earth.
7. Why did the Daleks plant Vargas on Kembel?
8. How did Ian Chesterton prevent the Daleks from detonating a bomb at the Earth's core when they invaded the planet in the mid 22nd century?
9. Who was the leader of the rebels of the Vulcan colony attacked by the Daleks?
10. Who learnt of the Master Plan of the Daleks and tried to warn Earth, but was exterminated by the Daleks on Kembel?
11. Why was the Doctor's knowledge of the future of the Daleks so valuable to Davros?
12. Why had the Daleks and the Movellans reached stalemate in their war with each other?
13. In their pursuit of the first Doctor and his companions, the Daleks landed on Aridius, where they presented the Aridians with an ultimatum. What was it?
14. Why did the Daleks come to the planet Spiridon?
15. How did Davros survive his 'extermination' at the hands of the Daleks?
16. Why did the Daleks want to be implanted with the Human Factor?
17. How did they hope to isolate the Human Factor?
18. When they arrived on Skaro, the first Doctor was keen to explore the Dalek City. Ian, however, insisted that they leave the planet and its possible dangers. As usual, the Doctor got his own way – how?

19. How did the Daleks intend to wipe out all life on Spiridon?
20. Name two of the Thals who accompanied Ian and Barbara on their journey into the Dalek City.

1. Why did the Doctor install a randomiser in the TARDIS?
2. The starliner which crashed on Alzarius had come from which planet?
3. What monster dwelt in the heart of the Power Complex on Skonnos?
4. Name two of the Minyans searching for the *P7E*.
5. When the Doctor and Romana visited Brighton, they missed the opening of the Pavilion. Where did the TARDIS materialise when the Doctor tried to take Leela to Brighton?
6. What evil force drew the spaceship *Hydrax* and officers Sharkey, McMillan and O'Connor into E-Space?
7. Which alien race constructed android copies of, amongst others, the Doctor, Sarah, Harry and Benton?
8. What are the Horda?
9. The Earth's solar system originally contained a fifth planet between Mars and Jupiter. What happened to it?
10. Why did Scaroth, in his guise as Count Scarlioni, steal the Mona Lisa from the Louvre? And what was the ultimate fate of the stolen painting?
11. Who was the last survivor of Zolfa-Thura?
12. How do the Usurians hope to gain power in the Galaxy?
13. Who was known as the 'Butcher of Brisbane'?
14. What was to be found in the Pyramids of Mars?
15. Who was the Morestran scientist who became infected with anti-matter poisoning on Zeta Minor and was eventually transformed into an 'Anti-Man'? What was the sacrifice the Doctor insisted the scientist was morally obliged to make?
16. Why were the Tharils of such importance to Rorvic and his crew on board the privateer?
17. For what special purpose was the Leisure Hive built?
18. On her one visit to Skaro, Romana was taken prisoner by the Daleks and used as a slave worker in the excavations of the Kaled City. How did she escape?
19. Who was Soldeed?
20. Who are the Shobogans, and where do they live?

1. Several of the Doctor's companions have joined him on his travels by stowing away on the TARDIS. Name two of them.
2. Which of the Doctor's companions was born on the planet Alzarius?
3. Ian Chesterton and Barbara Wright were originally unwilling companions of the Doctor and Susan. Why did they join the two time travellers in their wanderings in the TARDIS?
4. K9 was originally the robotic pet of which scientist?
5. Which of the Doctor's companions was a member of the Space Security Service and died in the destruction of the planet Kembel?
6. On which planet did the Doctor meet Vicki?
7. Why did Romana finally leave the Doctor?
8. Which of the Doctor's companions was described by one of her colleagues as being all brain and no heart?
9. The Queen of Peladon once received a lecture on women's liberation from which of the Doctor's companions?
10. Why was the first Doctor initially so taken with Dodo?
11. Which of the Doctor's companions was a member of a tribe of savages?
12. How did Jo defeat Azal the Daemon?
13. How did Jamie and Zoe return to their own times?
14. Which of the first Doctor's companions almost became 'guests of Madame Guillotine'?
15. Many of the Doctor's female companions have been noted for the power of their lungs! But whose amplified screams, in which adventure, actually destroyed a monster?

1. Which planet in the Isop Galaxy has been visited by the Doctor and his companions?
2. What was the original function of the Conscience of Marinus, and how did the Marinians improve upon this?
3. Who created a robot Doctor to destroy the Doctor and his companions?
4. When they were in the Gobi Desert without any water, what was the new source of water which saved the lives of the Doctor and his companions?
5. Where did the Doctor and his companions meet Count Dracula and Frankenstein's monster?
6. Which valuable metal was to be found in abundance on the planet of the Sensorites?
7. Why did Jano, leader of the Elders, urge the Savages to rebel against the Elders?
8. What was the true identity of Koquillion?
9. How did the Drahvins' and the Rills' spaceships come to be stranded on the doomed planet in Galaxy Four?
10. Who was the leader of the Moroks on Xeros?
11. In which adventure was Ian Chesterton tried and found guilty of murder?
12. What was unusual about the City of the Mechonoids?
13. Name two of the Menoptera whom the Doctor and his companions befriended and whose planet they helped to reclaim from the Animus.
14. The Doctor first met the Meddling Monk in Northumberland in 1066. Where did they next meet?
15. When the TARDIS crew had been miniaturised in *Planet of the Giants*, why was it literally a matter of life and death for Barbara to be returned to her normal size?
16. What was the planet Desperus used for?
17. With whom did Steven and Dodo play a deadly game of hopscotch?
18. Where did the Monoids hide the bomb with which they intended to destroy the Humans on the Ark?
19. Who was the last keeper of the Conscience of Marinus?
20. Where is the only place in the Universe where the Varga plant grows naturally?

UNIT

1. What do the initials UNIT stand for?
2. The third Doctor agreed to become UNIT's scientific advisor on one main condition. What was this?
3. What incident prompted the formation of UNIT?
4. UNIT HQ is built on the site of which old building?
5. Where and when did the Doctor first meet Lethbridge-Stewart?
6. Name the UNIT Medical Officer who treated the Doctor after his third regeneration.
7. Where is UNIT Central Command based?
8. Who first alerted UNIT to the strange goings-on at K'anpo's meditation centre?
9. Although the Doctor enjoyed a lengthy association with UNIT, only two of its uniformed personnel have ever accompanied him on a journey in the TARDIS. Name them.
10. Suspicious of the activities of Global Chemicals, the Brigadier sent one of his men to infiltrate the factory by posing as a man from the Ministry of Ecology. Who was he?
11. How did the Brigadier – much to the Doctor's disgust – 'solve' the problem of the Silurians?
12. Experimenting with his TARDIS on Earth, the third Doctor was flung into a parallel Universe where England was ruled by a military dictatorship. Who were this world's counterparts of the Brigadier and Liz Shaw?
13. Why was Captain Mike Yates discharged from UNIT?
14. Why did the Brigadier summon the Doctor back to Earth with the Space/Time Telegraph?
15. When Mike Yates was hypnotised by BOSS into killing the Doctor, how did the Doctor break BOSS's hold on him?

1. When the Krotons attacked the TARDIS, it protected itself by using the HADS. What is the HADS?
2. The Great Intelligence controlled the Yeti through Human intermediaries, but who built the original Yeti?
3. On what did the Atlanteans, encountered by the second Doctor, feed?
4. Which of the Doctor's companions succumbed to the Macra Terror?
5. Who was the leader of the Space Pirates whom the Doctor, Jamie and Zoe met?
6. The White Robots, who threatened the Doctor and his companions, were the servants of whom?
7. Who was the young woman who aided the Doctor and Jamie in their struggle with the Chameleons?
8. Around the middle of the 18th century, stories were told by ancient mariners of a terrifying monster in the North Sea. What was it?
9. Name the young member of the English aristocracy and the British lieutenant who helped the Doctor, Jamie and Zoe in their fight against the War Lord.
10. What was the 'Island of Death' on the planet Dulkis?
11. What was the main function of the ioniser, which was used during Earth's second ice age?
12. Who was the former colleague of Salamander who plotted to destroy him and seize his power for himself?
13. Why did the Doctor decide to visit Professor Travers when the TARDIS landed in London in the late 20th century?
14. Who was second-in-command of the Martian spaceship which was found in the ice during the second ice age?
15. Why was the TARDIS unable to dematerialise when the Doctor and Jamie landed on the *Silver Carrier*?
16. Eldrad was the evil Kastrian whom the fourth Doctor fought. But who was Eldred?
17. What does the word SIDRAT stand for?
18. In the adventure *The Mind Robber*, why was the TARDIS forced to materialise in the Land of Fiction?

19. Why did the Dominators attempt to destroy the planet Dulkis?
20. How were the Krotons on the planet of the Gonds finally destroyed?

1. When the Doctor first met him in 1066, how did the Meddling Monk propose to help King Harold win the Battle of Hastings?
2. Tlotoxl was the Aztec High Priest of Sacrifice whom the Doctor and his friends met in 15th-century Mexico. Who was the High Priest of Knowledge?
3. Who was the 'Sea Beggar'?
4. Name the two cavemen who were candidates for the leadership of the tribe of Gum when the TARDIS materialised in prehistoric times.
5. In which adventure were Steven and Dodo forced to perform 'The Ballad of the Last Chance Saloon'?
6. Who were the Human servants of Magnus Greel in 19th-century London?
7. Because of his association with Barbara, Ian was chosen to be leader of the Aztec army. Who was Ian's rival for the leadership who challenged him to a duel to the death?
8. Name the clan laird of the Doctor's companion Jamie.
9. When the TARDIS crew travelled back to the time of cavemen, how did they finally escape the tribe which was holding them prisoner?
10. When the TARDIS landed in 18th-century France, where were Ian, Susan and Barbara imprisoned?
11. Unlike his second incarnation, the first Doctor was totally unmusical. When the Emperor Nero commanded him to play the lyre for his guests, how did the Doctor convince those assembled that he was a great musician?
12. Who was the Greek slave who befriended Ian and spared his life in the gladiatorial arena?
13. What did the thief Ibrahim threaten to do to Ian if he did not surrender all his money?
14. Name the Mongol war-lord who tried to kill the first Doctor and his companions and to assassinate Kublai Khan.
15. In *The Myth Makers*, what was Zeus's travelling temple?

1. Who is the legendary founder of Time Lord civilisation?
2. What incident prompted the Time Lords to adopt their policy of non-interference in the affairs of other races?
3. The Time Lords found the War Lord guilty of terrible crimes and sentenced him to dematerialisation. What did they do to the War Lord's home planet?
4. Who was the first of Gallifrey's solar engineers, who detonated the supernova which gave the Time Lords the ability to conquer time?
5. What is the Eye of Harmony and where is it to be found?
6. Name the traitorous Time Lord who helped both the Vardans and the Sontarans when they invaded Gallifrey.
7. How many regenerations can a Time Lord have before he dies of old age?
8. Why did Omega swear revenge upon the Time Lords?
9. The Time Lords sent the Doctor to Skaro at the time of the Daleks' creation, and entrusted him with the task of fulfilling one of three options concerning the future development of the Daleks. What were these three options?
10. Why did the Time Lords sentence Morbius to death?
11. Who is Cardinal Borusa?
12. When the Time Lords sent the third Doctor his two previous incarnations to assist him in his battle with Omega, why was the first Doctor only able to help in an advisory capacity?
13. What is the Matrix?
14. Gallifrey is protected from alien invasion by the transduction barriers and the quantum force-field. Who created the quantum force-field?
15. The Doctor has often had to fight against renegade Time Lords. Name three of them.

1. Who was Sir Reginald Styles, and why did guerillas from the 22nd century want to kill him?
2. When the Silurians awoke from their 100-million-years' hibernation, how did they first plan to wipe out the Humans, who had taken over their planet?
3. What was the purpose of the Inferno Project?
4. When the second and third Doctors met him, what had happened to Omega's physical body?
5. How was Omega finally destroyed by the Doctors?
6. Why was Arcturus opposed to the planet Peladon's proposed membership of the Galactic Federation?
7. Who were known to the Spiders of Metebelis Three as the 'two-legs'?
8. What is a Drashig?
9. Who was the Time Warrior?
10. Azal was prepared to either destroy Earth, or bequeath his power to someone who would then rule the planet. To whom did the Daemon offer his power?
11. Why did the colonists whom the Doctor and Jo met on the planet of the Doomsday Weapon leave Earth in the first place?
12. Who was Torbis?
13. How were the killer dolls of the Nestenes activated?
14. When the Doctor visited Draconia in the 26th century, it was his second visit to that planet. Under what circumstances had he visited the planet five hundred years previously?
15. Who was Ky?
16. Name the Martian Commander who arrived on Peladon to take over that planet.
17. Why were the Axons so interested in the Doctor?
18. Who accidentally discovered the antidote to the Green Death? What was the antidote?
19. Name the two brothers who helped the Doctor in his fight against the Giant Spiders of Metebelis Three.
20. Why was the Great One of Metebelis Three so anxious to retrieve the blue crystal which the Doctor had taken from the planet some time before?

1. Which alien creatures launched an attack on London through its sewers?
2. How did the Ice Warriors plan to alter Earth's atmosphere before their planned invasion of the planet in the 21st century?
3. When the Great Intelligence invaded London with the Yeti, the Doctor devised a plan to defeat the Intelligence once and for all. What was his plan and why did it fail?
4. Why did the Kraals want to invade Earth?
5. In its plan to take over the world, what was WOTAN's first step?
6. In their second attempted invasion of Earth, the Nestenes intended to use plastic daffodils as their main weapon to create widespread panic. How were the daffodils designed to do this?
7. How did the Zygons plan to change Earth to make it suitable for colonisation?
8. Why was the Skarasen sent from Loch Ness down the Thames to London?
9. During the Yeti invasion of London, who was the Great Intelligence's main pawn?
10. Who was the army officer who hoped to ensure that Earth and the aliens who landed on Mars would never make any peaceful contact?
11. Why did the leaders of Operation Golden Age pluck dinosaurs from Earth's past and transport them to present-day London?
12. The Doctor foiled the attempts of Mandragora to conquer Earth in the late 15th century. When will Mandragora next be in a position to try again?
13. How was WOTAN destroyed?
14. Mondas was the long-lost sister planet of Earth. Why did it return to the Solar System?
15. How did the Doctor hope to prevent a seemingly inevitable war between Humans and Silurians?

1. After the Master's destruction of Logopolis, where did the Doctor continue the running of the Logopolitan Program?
2. How did the Doctor come to learn of the Vardans' plan to invade Gallifrey?
3. What is a Krynoid?
4. Who was the Chief Scientist of the Kraals who battled with the Doctor? How did he die?
5. When the Doctor and Romana landed on Chloris, they discovered what the Doctor took to be the remains of a giant egg shell. What was it?
6. Name the Commander of the Movellan force which landed on Skaro.
7. When the Doctor visited Karn, he found the members of the Sisterhood using their telekinetic powers to cause spaceships to crash on the planet's surface. Why were they doing this?
8. How did the Doctor finally defeat the Company on Pluto?
9. Name the Commander and two other Human members of the Sandminer crew.
10. Who was the prominent Egyptologist whose body was used by Sutekh?
11. Tigellan society is divided into two major sub-strata – the Savants and the Deons. What is the major difference between the two?
12. The Kastrians foresaw the possibility that Eldrad might one day return and lead them into eternal wars in the Galaxy. How did they insure against this eventuality?
13. Why was Leela banished from the Tribe of the Sevateem?
14. Who was Weng-Chiang?
15. What is the Skarasen?
16. How did Professor Kettlewell's robot become a Giant Robot?
17. Who summoned the Doctor and Adric to Traken?

18. Who was the leader of the Argolins when the Doctor and Romana visited Argolis?
19. What monster dwelt in the Black Pool on Zeta Minor?
20. What was the Horror of Fang Rock?

1. What was to be found in the junkyard at 76, Totter's Lane, London?
2. To avoid awkward questions, the Doctor has often used the alias of Doctor John Smith. Which of his companions, in which adventure, first gave him this name?
3. What were the Seeds of Death? What were the Seeds of Doom?
4. Unlike the Doctor's TARDIS, the chameleon circuit of the Master's TARDIS is fully operational. Give two of the disguises it has assumed.
5. What are the two intelligent races which inhabit Skaro?
6. The Doctor's TARDIS is a prime example of what kind of time/space capsule?
7. In which adventure did the Doctor and his friends witness the final destruction of Earth?
8. What is a robot's prime directive?
9. By what name is a Mark Three Travel Machine far better known?
10. The fourth Doctor travelled to Egypt to foil the plans of Sutekh the Osirian. This was not his first trip to that country, however. When did he first visit Egypt and which of his old enemies did he meet there?
11. Apart from the Time Lords, name one other race which can travel through time.
12. How can the Doctor's companions understand the languages of the alien races with whom they come into contact?
13. Where is the source of the TARDIS's power located?
14. The Doctor has often spoken about his 'guru' whom he knew as a young Gallifreyan. When he met him again on Earth, what identity had his mentor taken?
15. Match up the following aliens with their respective home planets:

The Kraals	Phaester Osiris
The Visians	Solos
The Marsh Spiders	Mars

Aggedor	Vortis
The Ice Warriors	Oseidon
Sutekh	Alzarius
The Mutants	Peladon
The Optera	Mira

1. The Key to Time was split into six separate segments, each of which possessed a different form. What were these forms?
2. Who gave the Doctor and Romana the task of finding and reassembling the six segments of the Key to Time?
3. Why was it necessary for the Doctor and Romana to reassemble the Key to Time?
4. What was the Tracer?
5. In their search for the six segments of the Key to Time, on which planet did the Doctor and Romana *first* locate the first segment?
6. Why did the Graff Vynda Ka wish to buy the planet Ribos from Garron?
7. When he learnt that Ribos was supposedly abundant in the mineral jethryk, how did the Graff Vynda Ka's plans change?
8. What monsters guarded the Sacred Relics of Ribos at night?
9. Who was Garron's partner-in-crime on Ribos?
10. Why was Binro of Ribos called the Heretic?
11. What was the Pirate Planet?
12. Queen Xanxia discovered the Pirate Captain half-dead after his ship had crashed, and she remade him. What was the name of the Captain's wrecked ship?
13. Why was the Pirate Captain's ransacking of planets so important to the survival of Queen Xanxia?
14. What was the reason for the periodical emergence of telepaths or Mentiads on the planet Zanak?
15. What was so unusual about the stone circle on Boscombe Moor?
16. Who was Professor Amelia Rumford?
17. Why did the Megara sentence the Doctor to death?
18. The Megara were travelling to the planet Diplos to preside over the trial of Cessair of Diplos. With what crimes was she charged?
19. What identity did Cessair assume on Earth in the 20th century?
20. From which planet in which star system do the Ogri come?

1. How was the Conscience of Marinus destroyed?
2. When the TARDIS landed in France in 1572, Steven went off on a tour of the sights of Paris. What did the Doctor do?
3. How did the Doctor and his companions escape from the City of the Mechonoids?
4. Which of the Doctor's companions received a telepathic message from the Sensorites when the TARDIS materialised in a spaceship in orbit around their planet?
5. Barbara and her Menoptera friends were forced by the Zarbi to work in a slave colony on Vortis. Where on the planet was this slave colony?
6. Who are the natural enemies of the Aridians?
7. How did the Doctor help the Rills to escape from the planet on which they were stranded?
8. Why did Barbara kill Vicki's pet, the Sand Beast?
9. How did the ruling caste on Jano's planet ensure that they would become a 'perfect' race?
10. What was the original function of WOTAN as envisaged by Professor Brett, its creator?
11. Which of his companions once tried to strangle the Doctor in the TARDIS?
12. When her first trip in the TARDIS took her to the Space Ark, where did Dodo insist she had landed?
13. How did Barbara succeed in destroying the Animus on Vortis?
14. Who lived on the planet Sense-Sphere?
15. After escaping the St Bartholomew's Day Massacre in 1572, the TARDIS materialised on Wimbledon Common, where Steven temporarily left the Doctor. Why?

1. Why did the Daleks return to Skaro to 'resurrect' Davros?

2. When the first Doctor met them, the Thals were a race of absolute pacifists, who even refused to fight with the Daleks when their very lives were at stake. How did Ian change their opinion?

3. The Daleks planned to implant Humans with the Dalek Factor. What, as the Doctor described it, was the Dalek Factor?

4. What was the supreme weapon of the Daleks in the 41st century?

5. Which of the Doctor's companions impersonated a Dalek so that the TARDIS crew could escape imprisonment on Skaro?

6. Who was the crippled scientist who developed a bomb to destroy the Daleks, and died when he exploded it in the presence of a group of Daleks?

7. After the Daleks and the Movellans were defeated on Skaro, what happened to Davros?

8. Which of the planets in our solar system did the Daleks intend to be the first to fall in accordance with their Master Plan?

9. Who was the Thal girl who led the attack on Davros's bunker?

10. The Daleks' supreme weapon in the 41st century was powered by the rarest mineral in the Universe. What was the mineral, and on which planet had it been mined?

11. Which Human did the Daleks implant with the Dalek Factor and turn into a Human Dalek?

12. Who was Davros's second-in-command who was eventually exterminated by the Daleks?

13. Why did a taskforce of Daleks travel back in time from the Earth of the 22nd century to the Earth of the 20th century?

14. Name two of the Thals whom the Doctor and Jo met on the planet Spiridon.

15. Who was the member of the Earth expedition to Exxilon who sided with the Daleks, but later turned against them and blew up their saucer with himself inside it?
16. How did the second Doctor succeed in destroying the Daleks who had taken over the Vulcan colony?
17. What did the Thal Alydon leave for the Doctor and his companions outside the TARDIS when it first visited Skaro?
18. In their flight from the Pursuer Daleks at the Festival of Ghana, which member of the TARDIS crew was accidentally left behind and followed her friends in the Daleks' own time machine?
19. What were the Dalek Emperor's plans for the Doctor when the two enemies finally met on Skaro?
20. Who was the leader of the Thals on Skaro when the first Doctor visited the planet who was later exterminated by the Daleks?

The Master

1. On his first visit to Earth, where did the Master's TARDIS materialise?
2. The Master took on various aliases when he was on Earth. Give two of them.
3. In the story *The Mind of Evil*, why did the Master plan to destroy the first World Peace Conference?
4. The Master, posing as a Cambridge professor, built a machine which could transmit objects through time. What was the name of this machine?
5. Why did the dying Master, unable to regenerate, return to his home planet of Gallifrey?
6. Who was the governor of the gaol on Earth in which the Master was imprisoned?
7. How did the Master and his Dalek superiors hope to provoke war between Earth and Draconia?
8. Why did the Sea Devils need the Master?
9. When the Doctor met the Master on Gallifrey, the Master had reached his final regeneration and was dying. How did he then succeed in achieving one more regeneration?
10. How was the Master instrumental in the destruction of Atlantis?
11. The Master was responsible for the deaths of Nyssa's stepmother, Kassia, and of her father, Tremas. How was he responsible for the destruction of her home world of Traken?
12. Why did the Master wish to control the Doomsday Machine?
13. After the destruction of Atlantis, how did the Master escape the wrath of Kronos?
14. After the Doctor defeated the Master on Gallifrey, where did the two Time Lords next meet?
15. In *Logopolis*, how did the Master attempt to hold the entire Universe to ransom?

1. Why was the Doctor exiled to Earth by the Time Lords?
2. Salamander hid a group of people underground who regularly caused 'natural' disasters on the Earth's surface. Why did they do this, and how did Salamander persuade them to remain underground for so long?
3. Why were the Space Pirates so interested in attacking space beacons?
4. Who were the Fish People whom the Doctor, Polly, Ben and Jamie met?
5. Professor Travers helped the Doctor in his fight against the Yeti in London. Where and when did the two friends first meet?
6. On what did the Weed Creature in *Fury from the Deep* feed?
7. Professor Watkins invented the Cerebratron Mentor machine which Tobias Vaughn planned to use against the Cybermen. What was the original function of the machine?
8. Who was the leader of the base which was attacked by Ice Warriors during Earth's second ice age?
9. What plans did the Master Brain, which controlled the Land of Fiction, have for the Doctor?
10. Who was Damon?
11. What was the name of the leader of the warrior monks of the Det-sen monastery who was killed by the abbot Songsen?
12. On which planet were the headquarters of the Issigri Mining Company?
13. How did the plans of Professor Zaroff threaten to destroy the entire world?
14. Who was the leader of the Gonds when the TARDIS landed on their planet?
15. Why did the Krotons need the 'high brains' of the Doctor and Zoe?

1. To which chapter of Time Lords does the Doctor belong?
2. What is the Celestial Intervention Agency?
3. The early Time Lords helped an alien race to progress, and as a result were looked upon by them as gods. Which race was this?
4. What is the Record of Rassilon?
5. The Elixir of Life, which was to be found on the planet Karn, was used by both the Sisterhood and the Time Lords. The Sisters used it to gain eternal life. Why did the Time Lords use it?
6. What was the ultimate weapon, powered by the Great Key of Rassilon, which was constructed by the Time Lady Rodan, under hypnosis and following the instructions of K9?
7. The Time Lords exiled the Doctor to Earth for an indefinite period of time. Why did they finally release him from his exile?
8. When the Master escaped from Gallifrey after a failed attempt to destroy his home planet, it was thought that he took the Great Key of Rassilon with him. What really became of the Great Key?
9. What unanticipated advantage did the Doctor's destruction of Omega have for the Time Lords?
10. Name the member of the High Council of the Time Lords who betrayed Gallifrey to the Master.
11. What is the First Law of Time, and how and when did the Time Lords break it?
12. Rodan was a Gallifreyan who befriended Leela. What was her job in the Capitol?
13. Although the fourth Doctor often fought with evil Time Lords, the first Doctor only ever met one. Who was it?
14. How did the Time Lords win their bitter war with the Giant Vampires and destroy all but one of their number?

15. Linked with the Matrix, the Sash of Rassilon, the Rod of Rassilon and the Great Key provide the total sum of all Time Lord power. How did Rassilon ensure that no President of the Time Lords should ever use this power to establish an evil dictatorship?

1. Why did Eric Klieg awaken the dormant Cybermen in their tombs?
2. The Commanding Officer of the Snowcap Tracking Station planned to destroy the planet Mondas with the Z-Bomb. Why did the first Doctor object to this plan?
3. How did the Doctor try to use a Cybermat to defeat the Cybermen on Nerva?
4. Who was the leader of the Moonbase, which was attacked by the Cybermen in the year 2070?
5. How did the Cybermen spread the 'plague' which was sweeping Space Beacon Nerva?
6. Who was the Human who performed the astonishing feat of destroying a Cyberman with his bare hands?
7. When their planet was in danger of being attacked by the Z-Bomb, how did the Cybermen ensure that the Earthmen would remove the warhead from the rocket?
8. Why were the Cybermen themselves unable to perform this task?
9. How did Polly succeed in destroying the group of Cybermen who had taken over the Moonbase in 2070?
10. When the Cybermen failed to destroy Voga with three cobalt bombs strapped to the backs of their prisoners, what alternative plan did they adopt?
11. In which adventure did the Cybermats make their first appearance?
12. How did the second Doctor succeed in protecting himself and his friends from the hypnotic forces of the Cybermen when they invaded Earth in the late 20th century?
13. How was the main fleet of Cybermen on the Moon finally defeated?
14. Name the Earthman who was in league with both the Vogans and the Cybermen when the Cybermen returned to the Solar System after the great Cyberwar.
15. Who was the leader of the archaelogical expedition to the tomb of the Cybermen? Who financed the expedition?

16. Why did the Cybermen take over the Wheel in Space?
17. How did the Vogans finally destroy the Cybermen who had come to their planet?
18. How did the Cybermen introduce a 'space plague' on the Moonbase in the year 2070?
19. Why did the Cybermen who had invaded the Snowcap Ice Base die?
20. Why has Earth been a target for several invasion attempts by the Cybermen?

1. Who were the Ambassadors of Death?
2. Why were the mines of Peladon of such great importance in the war between the Galactic Federation and Galaxy Five?
3. Who was Cho-je?
4. The Time Lords sent the Doctor and Jo to Solos with a box which would only open for its intended recipient. Who was the box for, and what did it contain?
5. How did the renegade Ice Warriors and the traitor Eckersley ensure that the Federation mining operations on Peladon were disrupted?
6. What was in the ancient barrow opened at Devil's End?
7. Who was the Exxilon who accompanied the Doctor on his journey into the heart of the Exxilon City?
8. What was the temporal paradox in which the guerillas who came from the 22nd century to kill Sir Reginald Styles found themselves caught?
9. Who was Professor Sondergaard?
10. How did Kalik plan to wrest power on Inter Minor from his brother President Zarb?
11. Where was the Doctor intending to take Sarah for a holiday when the TARDIS materialised on Exxilon?
12. Who was the leader of the colonists on the planet of the Doomsday Machine, Exarius, who gave his life for his fellow colonists?
13. Name the two Overlord guards who helped the Doctor and Jo on Solos.
14. Which of the Federation technicians who had come to supervise mining operations on Peladon was killed by a fake Aggedor?
15. How were the Giant Spiders of Metebelis Three brought to Earth?
16. Who was Captain Dent?
17. Name the Spiridon who cured Jo Grant of a deadly fungus disease and sacrificed himself to save his home planet.

18. Who were the reptile men discovered in underground hibernation chambers on Earth?
19. The planet of the Ogrons is a bleak and uninviting planet at the edge of the Galaxy. What other creature shares the planet with the Ogrons?
20. Why was the third Doctor forced to regenerate?

1. Who was the Queen Mother of France when the Doctor and Steven visited that country?
2. Scaroth of the Jagaroth constantly influenced Mankind's development throughout the centuries. What was his ultimate purpose in doing this?
3. While playing a game of backgammon, the Doctor put up the TARDIS as a stake – and lost! To whom did he lose?
4. Name the astrologer at the court of San Martino who was the leader of the Brethren of Demnos, and was taken over by Mandragora.
5. How did King Richard I hope to make a peace between himself and Saladin?
6. With whom did Troilus and Cressida go to build another Troy?
7. The *Marie Celeste*, which was found floating at sea, deserted by its crew, has remained a mystery for years. According to *Doctor Who*, what really happened?
8. What reason did Tlotoxl, the Aztecs' High Priest of Sacrifice, have for denouncing Barbara as a false goddess?
9. Why did people believe that the monastery of the Meddling Monk was occupied by a brotherhood of monks when only one had ever been seen?
10. Which of the Doctor's companions was chosen to marry the Perfect Victim?
11. The first Doctor was mistaken for Maximus Pettulian, a famous Corinthian lyrist, who was supposedly on his way to Rome to entertain the Emperor Nero. What was Maximus Pettulian's real intention?
12. Steven succeeded in entering Troy by deliberately picking a fight with Paris and being taken prisoner. What name did he assume in Troy?
13. Why did the Clanton family threaten to lynch Steven when the TARDIS arrived in Tombstone in 1881?
14. What did the crooked solicitor Grey intend to do with his Scottish prisoners when the Doctor visited Scotland in 1746?

15. The Doctor has often given Earth history a push in the right direction. He gave the Greeks the idea of the Trojan Horse and (if we can believe him!) helped Isaac Newton by dropping an apple on his head! How did he give the Emperor Nero the idea of burning Rome?

1. Who imprisoned the Doctor and Romana in a Chronic Hysteresis?
2. Why did Xoanon become insane?
3. The zoologist Tryst invented the CET machine, otherwise known as the Continuous Event Transmitter. What was it and why did it go wrong on the space cruiser *Empress*?
4. When the Doctor, Sarah and Harry first landed on Nerva during the attack of the Wirrrn, it was being used as a space ark. What was its original function?
5. Fetch Priory was the scene of which *Doctor Who* adventure?
6. Why did Erato come to the planet Chloris?
7. According to the Doctor, who knitted his long multi-coloured scarf?
8. Who ruled the Alzarians on board the Starliner?
9. From which neighbouring planet did Skonnos demand tribute of Hymetusite crystals?
10. Why was the Doctor so important to the schemes of Doctor Solon?
11. What did Moberley and Winlett of Antarctica Camp Three find buried in the Antarctic perma-frost?
12. Who were the Sunmakers?
13. When Styre landed on Earth, he found an uninhabited world. Why had Earth been evacuated?
14. What was the Oracle?
15. Out of which substance was Rorvik's privateer constructed? Why?
16. What was the true identity of Professor Chronotis whom the Doctor and Romana met at Cambridge?
17. How did the Doctor destroy the Great Vampire?
18. When the Doctor and Romana visited Paris in 1979, how did they first become aware that someone was interfering with time?
19. Who was Taren Capel?
20. When the Wirrrn Queen arrived on the Space Ark Nerva, she was killed by the Ark's automatic defence system, but not before she laid her eggs. Where exactly did she lay them?

1. In her first incarnation, Romana was the double of which Taran princess?
2. Which branch of Taran society was particularly skilled in the construction of androids?
3. During the Doctor and Romana's visit to Tara, Count Grendel of Gracht tried twice to take the Taran throne. How did he make his first attempt, and how was it thwarted by the Doctor?
4. Who was Madame Lamia?
5. Why were the Tarans forced to develop the science of building androids?
6. How did Count Grendel intend to use Romana to help him win the throne of Tara?
7. Kroll was the gigantic squid-like god of the Swampies on Delta Three. How did he achieve his gigantic size?
8. What was the function of the refinery on Delta Three?
9. The original home of the Swampies was Delta Magna. Why were they living on Delta Three when the Doctor and Romana landed there?
10. Who were the Sons of Earth? And which of their number was a member of the Refinery team on Delta Three?
11. What awoke Kroll from his deep sleep on Delta Three?
12. Kroll was totally blind. How then did he hunt?
13. Rohm Dutt was a gun-runner who supplied arms to the Swampies. Who gave him this commission and why?
14. To whom did the Black Guardian entrust the task of seizing the Key to Time?
15. What is the sister planet of Zeos?
16. Who built the super-computer Mentalis, which the Doctor and Romana found on Zeos?
17. What was the Armageddon Factor?
18. Who effectively ruled Atrios during its war with Zeos?
19. During his search for the final segment to the Key to Time, the Doctor was obliged to make a time loop. Why and how did he do this?

20. After the Doctor had assembled the Key to Time and
    defeated the Black Guardian's servant, how did the
    Black Guardian attempt to seize the Key?

The Sontarans and the Rutans

1. Why did the Sontarans invade Gallifrey?
2. What was the bargain which Linx struck with Irongron in the Middle Ages?
3. What is a Sontaran's only weak point?
4. Why did the Rutans come to Earth in the early 20th century?
5. Who killed Linx?
6. Why did Linx, stranded in Earth's Middle Ages, kidnap scientists from the 20th century?
7. Which alien race did the Sontarans use in their invasion of Gallifrey?
8. Why did the Doctor challenge Styre to single unarmed combat?
9. What use to a Sontaran is his probic vent?
10. What Human form did the Rutan scout take when it visited the Channel coast in the early 20th century?
11. Who was the leader of the Sontarans who invaded Gallifrey?
12. Why did the Sontarans wish to invade Earth, which had been rendered uninhabitable by solar flares?
13. Name the home planet of the Rutans.
14. When the Rutan scout arrived at Fang Rock in the early 20th century, how did it isolate the island?
15. After the defeat of the Rutan scout at Fang Rock, how did the Doctor destroy the approaching Rutan spaceship?

1. Why was the Skarasen so necessary to the Zygons' survival?
2. How was the second Krynoid destroyed?
3. Why was the Doctor mortally feared by the Sevateem and, initially at least, honoured by the Tesh?
4. What and where was the Bi-Al Foundation?
5. Why were the mineral samples found on Zeta Minor so important to Morestra? And why was it impossible for the Morestrans to take the samples back to their home planet?
6. What did the Nimon promise to the people of Skonnos in return for providing him with Hymetusite crystals?
7. Why did the Doctor decide to go to Logopolis?
8. Who was the leader of the Outlers on Alzarius?
9. Distinguish between the following: the Fendahl; the Fendahl Core; the Fendahleen.
10. Who was the Commander of the Space Ark Nerva when the Doctor, Sarah and Harry arrived there? After he was taken over by the Wirrrn, who replaced him as Commander?
11. When the Eye of Horus was destroyed, Sutekh was still imprisoned in Egypt for two minutes, which gave the Doctor enough time to devise a means of defeating the Osirian. Explain how this was possible.
12. Condo was the servant of Solon on Karn. How did Solon guarantee his continued service?
13. Who was the leader of the resistance movement against the Company on Pluto?
14. What is the sister planet of Zolfa-Thura?
15. Who was Madam Karela?
16. What lay at the core of the planet into which the Minyan probe vessel crashed?
17. The Mandrels are ferocious beasts who live on the planet Eden. Why are they so important to drug smugglers?
18. In their fight against Scaroth, who was the private detective who helped the Doctor and Romana?

19. Who were the two Security Agents for the Company on board the Sandminer? And why were they there?
20. What in reality was the castle of King Zargo?

1. Liz Shaw was a scientist at which English university?
2. Which of the Doctor's companions was the handmaiden of the prophetess Cassandra and sacrificed herself to save the Doctor from the Daleks?
3. Jo was given the chance to become Queen of which planet?
4. Susan, the Doctor's granddaughter, left him to begin a new life with a freedom fighter who had helped to free Earth from the power of the Daleks. What was his name?
5. Steven left the Doctor to lead which race of aliens?
6. The Doctor revealed in *Frontier in Space* that he was a nobleman of the planet Draconia. Which of his companions was made a knight by King Richard I?
7. Which of his companions did the Doctor return to Earth on the very day they had left?
8. With the exception of Susan, who was the Doctor's first companion not to have been born on Earth?
9. Which of the Doctor's companions was a doctor in the Navy?
10. Why did the Mark One version of K9 remain on Gallifrey?
11. Why did the Doctor return Sarah to Earth?
12. The Doctor is notorious for often being unable to steer his TARDIS correctly. How then did Ian and Barbara finally return to the London of their own time?
13. Why was it necessary for K9 to stay behind with Romana in E-Space?
14. Which of the Doctor's companions was an Australian air hostess until she joined the Doctor on his travels?
15. With the exception of Romana, name any two of the Doctor's companions who have visited Gallifrey.

1. Why did Davros believe the Daleks to be the force not of evil but of good?
2. Why did the Daleks imprison Victoria, the daughter of Edward Waterfield?
3. Why were the Thals, led by Temmosus, forced to make a journey to the Dalek City?
4. While escaping the Mechonoid City, which had just been invaded by the Daleks, what did the Doctor deliberately leave behind for the Daleks?
5. How did the Daleks, aided by the Meddling Monk, hope to persuade the Doctor to hand over to them the core of their Time Destructor?
6. Ronson helped the Doctor and his friends to halt the evil experiments of Davros. Who was Ronson?
7. How did the Daleks procure the aid of Theodore Maxtible?
8. When the Daleks invaded Earth for the first time, where in England did they establish their mines?
9. How was the Doctor able to guide his erratic TARDIS to Kembel to confront the Daleks?
10. Which of the TARDIS crew did the Daleks attempt to convert into a Roboman? Why?
11. When the Doctor was sent back in time to prevent the Dalek's creation, he failed to do so, but nevertheless did achieve one small victory. What was it?
12. How did the Doctor defeat the Dalek army on Spiridon?
13. How did the Doctor escape being turned into a Human Dalek when he was brought to Skaro by the Daleks?
14. With which individual did the Daleks ally themselves in their attempts to provoke a space war in the year 2540?
15. How did the Doctor destroy the Daleks on the planet Kembel?

1. What is the Dodecahedron?
2. How did Magnus Greel hope to halt his cellular destruction?
3. Which planet had the Nimon devastated immediately before they turned their attention to Skonnos?
4. How did the Doctor finally defeat and kill Sutekh?
5. When the Doctor, Leela and K9 arrived on Pluto, they found a relatively warm planet. How had the Company achieved this?
6. Who was the missing Earth astronaut who was deceived into aiding the Kraals in their planned invasion of Earth?
7. Why did the Brethren of Demnos, controlled by the Mandragora Helix, deem it necessary to kill the guests at the masque held in honour of the new Duke of San Martino?
8. After Xoanon was restored to sanity, the Tesh and the Sevateem thought it wise to unite. Who was suggested as their leader?
9. Why and how did the Tythonians plan to destroy Chloris and its solar system?
10. Who was the leader of the Shobogans whom Leela met?
11. In his quest for abundant supplies of quartz, the Pirate Captain turned his attention to Earth. How did the Doctor and Romana prevent him from destroying Earth?
12. Who was the Argolin who attempted to duplicate himself into an army to wage another war on the Foamasi?
13. In *The Deadly Assassin*, the Doctor was sentenced to vaporisation by the Time Lords. How did he achieve forty-eight hours' grace?
14. Who was the head of the Logopolis Program when the Doctor visited that planet?
15. How was the Nucleus and its Swarm finally destroyed?
16. How did the Doctor defeat Taren Capel?

17. Name the young Trog whose father the Doctor saved from being killed by the Seers of the Oracle.
18. What were the names of the two spaceships which 'crashed' into each other when leaving hyper-space en route to the planet Azure?
19. What was the connexion between the Marsh Spiders, the Marshmen and the crew of the Starliner whom the Doctor and Romana met on Alzarius?
20. Why was the fourth Doctor forced to regenerate?

1. Who was (a) the Watcher whom the first Doctor met, and (b) the Watcher who played a vital role in *Logopolis*?
2. Why can no one unlock the TARDIS door with the key unless the Doctor so wishes?
3. What was the Whomobile?
4. Which of the following is the odd one out, and why? Quarks; Daleks; K9; Polyphase Avatron; Gundans; Mechonoids; Chumblies.
5. What was the 'Dead Planet'?
6. What is the Time Vector Generator of the TARDIS, and in which adventure, and why, was it disconnected?
7. What are the two social castes of Martians?
8. K9 was the fourth Doctor's robotic dog. But who was K1?
9. Which planet in Earth's own solar system is particularly abundant in the mineral trisilicate?
10. What are 'corpse-markers'?
11. When Eldrad entered the Doctor's TARDIS, he was unable to harm the Doctor or Sarah. Why would it be impossible for any enemy to harm the Doctor in the TARDIS control room?
12. What is Shada?
13. Mars, the fourth planet from our Sun, is a dead world. What caused this devastation, and who made Mars habitable again for humans?
14. What are T-Mat and Trans-mat?
15. Why are TARDISes bigger inside than outside?

Behind the Scenes

1. Name all the actors who have played the Doctor.
2. Who wrote the very first *Doctor Who* story in 1963?
3. The actor Nicholas Courtney played the part of Lethbridge-Stewart during the reigns of the second, third and fourth Doctors. What role did he play opposite the first Doctor?
4. When was the first episode of *Doctor Who* broadcast?
5. Who composed the *Doctor Who* theme music?
6. In the 1980 adventure *Meglos*, the actress Jacqueline Hill played the part of the Deon Lexa. Which other role had she played in *Doctor Who* years before?
7. Who wrote the very first Dalek story, and has continued to write most of the Dalek stories ever since?
8. What was the name of the adventure in which the fifth Doctor made his first appearance?
9. The role of the Master has been played by several actors over the years. Name them.
10. Who has been the longest-serving script-editor ever of the *Doctor Who* television series, and has also written most of the Target novelisations of the Doctor's adventures?
11. What was *Doctor Who and the Seven Keys to Doomsday*?
12. Which *Doctor Who* script-editor and writer has written a highly successful radio and televison series about a group of galactic hitch-hikers?
13. Which actress who played one of the Doctor's companions later went on to become a star in the television series *Upstairs, Downstairs*?
14. Who was the first producer of *Doctor Who*?
15. Name the two actors who have supplied the voice of K9.
16. Which two famous British satirists found themselves in a Paris art gallery, admiring the exquisite beauty of a certain London police box which, much to their delight, suddenly vanished into thin air?
17. Which actor played the part of Andrews, a naval officer trapped in Vorg's Scope, in the 1973 adventure *Carnival*

of Monsters, returned several years later to play a regular role in the television series, and is now the author of several Target novelisations of *Doctor Who* stories?

18. What was the name of the team of stunt men who played a major role in the early adventures of the third Doctor?

19. Which of the actors who have played the role of the Doctor first became well known for his portrayal of a slightly incompetent Yorkshire vet?

20. Match the following actresses with the characters they have played in *Doctor Who*:

Caroline John	Vicki
Lalla Ward	Katarina
Anneke Wills	Leela
Adrienne Hill	Dodo
Louise Jameson	Polly
Jackie Lane	Liz Shaw
Maureen O'Brien	Zoe
Wendy Padbury	Romana (second incarnation)

THE ANSWERS

1. Time And Relative Dimensions In Space.
2. Because he was bored with the Time Lord life style and wanted to observe the Universe at first hand.
3. Mutters Spiral.
4. Invisibility.
5. 51% (a double gamma).
6. The Ice Warriors.
7. *Fury from the Deep*.
8. A Charged Vacuum Emboitement, leading into other universes, such as E-Space, and used by the Logopolitans to preserve our Universe beyond its point of natural heat-death.
9. The Ogri; Eldrad the Kastrian.
10. Skaro.
11. The Rutans.
12. Susan, the Doctor's granddaughter.
13. The Master's.
14. *The Mind Robber*.
15. Gallifrey.

1. The Daleks.
2. Ian taught science and Barbara taught history.
3. Survivors from an Earth spaceship had contaminated the Sensorites' drinking water with deadly nightshade.
4. The Menoptera.
5. 'The Traveller from beyond Time'.
6. Arbitan possessed one in the pyramid on Marinus; the second was in the city of Morphoton; the third in the laboratory of Darrius in the midst of the Screaming Jungle; the fourth in a cavern frozen in a block of ice; and the fifth in the city of Millenius.
7. The 'fast return' switch, which the Doctor had activated to take Ian and Barbara back to their own time, had jammed.
8. The roof of the Space Ark.
9. Marc Cory.
10. To use gliders, launched by catapults.
11. The Animus.
12. He removed the Dimensional Control of the Monk's TARDIS.
13. Koquillion (Bennett in disguise).
14. Themselves as 'living' exhibits in the Moroks' Space Museum.
15. The Will Operating Thought Analogue machine, Professor Brett's computer which attempted to conquer the world.
16. The Hearts Family.
17. Leader of the Drahvins who were stranded on a planet in Galaxy Four.
18. Refusis.
19. His sister, Sara Kingdom, who believed he was a traitor.
20. Cameca.

1. Dodo Chaplet; Tegan Jovanka.
2. Romanadvoratrelundar.
3. Leela.
4. She was brought by the Watcher.
5. Jamie.
6. Jo Grant.
7. *Metropolitan.*
8. Latep; on Skaro.
9. Coal Hill Secondary School, London.
10. Zoe.
11. Mechanus.
12. The Harris family.
13. Ben Jackson.
14. Princess Astra of Atrios.
15. Vicki.

1. The Chameleons, aliens who took over the identities of Humans.
2. By the Gravitron.
3. Astrid Ferrier.
4. With torrential rain.
5. Padmasambhava.
6. Ben.
7. A would-be world dictator who was also the Doctor's double.
8. He intended to employ the survivors of these wars as an invincible army to take over the Galaxy.
9. Ta (in the Pliny solar system).
10. Three ('Alpha', 'Beta' and 'Omega').
11. To form itself into a vast colony to take over the British Isles and, in time, perhaps the whole planet.
12. An Ice Warrior found frozen in the ice during Earth's second ice age.
13. Covent Garden Underground Station.
14. Its automatic defence network (accidentally triggered by the Doctor) tried to 'tempt' the time travellers away from the rocket by showing them seductive scenes of other planets.
15. An atmospheric imbalance caused by the decrease of carbon dioxide in the atmosphere.
16. Jarvis Bennet.
17. By showing them images of their own homes on the scanner.
18. Kemel.
19. Because it was only high mental power which could reanimate them.
20. The War Lords.

1. The Kaleds of Skaro (in the first Dalek story they were referred to as Dals).
2. The Dalek Emperor.
3. Davros.
4. A neutron bomb exploded in the bitter war between the Thals and the Kaleds.
5. Draconia.
6. By their experiments in time travel using static electricity.
7. The Ogrons.
8. Mavic Chen.
9. The Mechonoids.
10. (a) To cure those on the Earth colonies who had become infected.
    (b) To hold Earth to ransom.
11. Through the space/time visualiser which the Doctor was given on Xeros.
12. To destroy the Thal survivors on Skaro, and to make life on Skaro more suitable for the Daleks, who had become accustomed to the radioactivity in the planet's atmosphere.
13. In preparation for their invasion of the Galaxy.
14. By developing a powerful anti-radiation drug.
15. Lesterson.
16. By introducing the Human Factor to some Daleks, so making them question their Black Dalek masters.
17. To remove the Earth's core and replace it with a drive mechanism in order to pilot the planet through the Universe.
18. Because they considered him to be an inferior being and of no further use to them.
19. By introducing a space plague, brought to Earth by 'meteorites'.
20. Because he believed that even the Daleks are a force for good: without the Dalek threat, many planets would war amongst themselves, rather than unite to fight the Daleks.

1. In the middle of a forest clearing in Oxley Woods on Earth.
2. Aggedor.
3. Giant maggots and the Green Death.
4. The Beacon of the City of the Exxilons.
5. They believed that a rogue planet would take away Earth's atmosphere for a time. (It did not: the planet settled into orbit around Earth and became the Moon.)
6. With guns hidden in either their hands or their wrists.
7. On the Moon.
8. Vorg and Shirna.
9. He considered Earth to be an experiment that had failed.
10. Thalira, his daughter.
11. Because General Carrington tricked them into believing that they would be welcomed as ambassadors.
12. The Master.
13. The blue crystal from Metebelis Three. She returned it because of the fear it inspired in the natives accompanying her husband and herself down the Amazon.
14. Bessie.
15. Metebelis Three. The TARDIS materialised in the hold of the SS *Bernice*, an exhibit in Vorg's Scope, which he had just brought to Inter Minor.
16. A revolutionary method of reforming hardened criminals by extracting the evil from their minds. It was the invention of Professor Keller (the Master).
17. With nuclear power drawn from the Inferno Project.
18. Anat, Boaz and Shura.
19. Hepesh.
20. The City of the Exxilons.

1. With a metal virus, invented by Professor Kettlewell.
2. Zargo, Camilla and Aukon, the servants of the Great Vampire in E-Space.
3. By making heat available to the Universe by opening CVEs into other universes.
4. Broton.
5. Salt.
6. Dums, Vocs and a Super-Voc.
7. Maren.
8. Paris.
9. A lost Minyan spaceship; the Minyans were searching for it because it contained the vital race banks of the Minyans.
10. The time travel experiment of Magnus Greel, who escaped justice in the 51st century by travelling back in time to the 19th century.
11. The Collector.
12. The Master, using the power he had gained from temporarily being Keeper of Traken, took over his body.
13. The Sontarans.
14. King Rokon.
15. Argolis.
16. To test Human resistance to a Sontaran invasion of the Galaxy.
17. It hijacked the TARDIS.
18. Because by offering Chloris metal in exchange for chlorophyll, he was threatening Adrasta's monopoly of metal on the planet. His presence in the pit also discouraged any raiders in Adrasta's mines.
19. The fourth Doctor's.
20. Vraxoin ('vrax'). Tryst found it on Eden.

1. Za.
2. King Richard I.
3. Giuliano.
4. He lined the castle ramparts with dummy figures of soldiers to give the impression that the castle was well defended. When Irongron's men saw through this, he frightened them away with home-made fireworks.
5. The Abbot of Amboise.
6. Algernon Ffinch.
7. That the Greeks would leave Troy a gift which would prove the city's doom. She thought this gift was the TARDIS – it was, of course, the Trojan Horse, an idea which the Doctor suggested to the Greeks!
8. To obtain the Khan's permission to return to Venice.
9. Because she was wearing Yetaxa's bracelet, which she had picked up in his tomb.
10. Saladin.
11. An English counter-revolutionary.
12. Samuel Pike.
13. Doc Holliday.
14. It was suggested that the Doctor's next companion, Dodo, whose surname was Chaplet and whose grandfather was French, may have been descended from Anne.
15. The Meddling Monk; the Daemons; the Mandragora Helix; the Fendahl; the Exxilons; Scaroth of the Jagaroth

1. Humans, controlled by the Daleks and used by them to rule their other Human slaves.
2. Two days.
3. The Celestial Toymaker.
4. A part-animal, part-vegetable creature, resembling a cactus and native to Skaro. Infection from a Varga attacks the brain until one is transformed into another Varga. Marc Cory and his crew found a colony of Vargas on Kembel.
5. The Menoptera; the Zarbi; the Optera; the Venom Grubs or Larvae Guns.
6. Earth became involved in interplanetary wars and Mechanus was forgotten.
7. Polly.
8. A stone sarcophagus.
9. The space/time visualiser.
10. Marinus.
11. Farrow, aware of the dangers of DN6, announced that Forester would have to give up his research into DN6.
12. Because they wanted no one to leave their planet and reveal the existence of its vast resources of Molybdenum.
13. A vicious monster used by the Daleks to guard their mines on Earth in the 22nd century.
14. Zeus (in the guise of an old beggar!).
15. Chumblies.
16. The Humans had now become the slaves of the Monoids; Dodo, who had infected the Ark with her cold, was responsible.
17. He killed the crew of the spaceship because they had arrested him for murder; he spared Vicki because, unaware that he had committed a murder, she would provide a convincing alibi when they returned to Earth.
18. Captain Maitland.
19. To be objects of study in their zoo.
20. Yartek.

1. They were originally humanoids who gradually replaced old and diseased limbs with metal and plastic. Finally they even dispensed with emotions and became monstrous silver beings intent on achieving power and domination over the Universe.
2. Mondas and Telos.
3. With Professor Watkins' Cerebratron Mentor machine.
4. Small, silvery, rat-like creatures used by the Cybermen.
5. Voga. The Humans used Voga's gold to destroy the Cybermen.
6. Telos.
7. To take them back to Mondas and turn them into Cybermen.
8. By using the Gravitron to drastically alter the Earth's weather.
9. By detonating a Cyber megatron bomb which would destroy all life on Earth.
10. The plan failed when the radio transmitter on Earth, whose radio waves the Cybermen were homing in on, was destroyed. The Cyberfleet was then destroyed with nuclear warheads.
11. To destroy Voga.
12. General Cutler.
13. It was unable to contain all the energy it had drained from Earth.
14. All International Electromatics equipment had special Cyber circuits built into them. The Cybermen's plan was to activate these circuits which would then put the Humans into a deep hypnotic trance.
15. By homing in on their brainwaves.
16. They were needed to carry three deadly cobalt bombs down to the core of Voga to destroy the planetoid. The Cybermen were unable to perform this task because the heart of Voga was made of almost pure gold.
17. Mondas.
18. Krail and Krang.
19. On the dark side of the Moon.

20. They ionised a star, thus causing meteorites to strike the Wheel. The Cybermats, meanwhile, had consumed the Wheel's supplies of bernalium, without which the Wheel was unable to deflect the meteorites. The only place where bernalium could be found was on the *Silver Carrier*.

1. Because he needed their help in sending all the soldiers who had been kidnapped by the War Lord and his people back to their own time zones on Earth.
2. By sending to Gallifrey a small cube, into which he had telepathically placed all the necessary data about what had happened.
3. That the Doctor should look after Victoria, his daughter.
4. Amdo.
5. The Master Brain, a computer.
6. The Cybermen.
7. The Quarks.
8. To lure the Doctor and Jamie into the clutches of the Daleks, and to ensure the Doctor's co-operation in the schemes of the Dalek Emperor.
9. The Mexican revolutionary who was captured and used by the War Lord.
10. With the ioniser.
11. A spaceship in the Kroton battle fleet.
12. To act as a radio-visual relay station for Earth; as a half-way house for deep-space ships; as a research station; and as an early-warning station for all kinds of space phenomena.
13. Dom Issigri.
14. King Thous.
15. For an Examiner from Earth.
16. Madeleine Issigri.
17. To save it from a group of Chinese bandits who were attacking the monastery.
18. He was ejected into time and space when he tried to steal the TARDIS.
19. The Intelligence said that it wished to attempt to create substance for itself. It did not tell Padmasambhava that its real intention was to overwhelm and conquer the world.
20. By cutting off the supplies of toxic gas on which the Macra were dependent.

1. Tobias Vaughn.
2. It would destroy all insect life on Earth and so upset the delicate balance of the planet's ecology.
3. Because it foresaw a time when Earth might pose a threat to it.
4. By destroying the Van Allen Belt.
5. They claimed that their fuel system had been exhausted and they needed to rest a while to replenish their energy cycles. They had really come to drain Earth of all its energy.
6. The explosion of the Jagaroth spaceship sparked off the chemical reaction which eventually produced all life on Earth. If Scaroth had succeeded in preventing the explosion, the Human race would never have existed!
7. The sending of two 'meteorite' swarms to Earth (in reality containers for the Nestene Consciousness).
8. Because they discovered that their planet had been destroyed in a solar explosion.
9. Marshal Chedaki.
10. Harrison Chase.
11. Lupton.
12. Because their home planet was a dying world.
13. With a deadly virus.
14. To roll back time and to take Earth back to a pollution-free Golden Age.
15. Sir Charles Grover was the minister, Professor Whitaker was the scientist.
16. The killer Autons were used to spread fear and panic throughout the country, while the Replicas, doubles of important figures in authority, helped to confuse the situation.
17. The eventual destruction of Earth and the emergence of Primords.
18. London.
19. To create a race of machines similar to itself.
20. With UHF radio waves.

1. Kronos the Chronavore.
2. Izlyr from Mars, with Ssorg as his assistant; Alpha Centauri; Arcturus; and Amazonia from Earth. (The Doctor and Jo were originally thought to be, respectively, the Earth delegate and a royal observer.)
3. The Draconians.
4. By trapping Axos in a time loop.
5. The Crystal of Kronos.
6. Hal.
7. It accelerated their natural evolutionary development, turning them into mutants.
8. Because many years ago the planet had been swept by a space plague, introduced by an alien visitor.
9. By draining all their power through a black hole, in preparation for his coming to Gallifrey and ruling the Time Lords.
10. The Guardian of the Doomsday Machine.
11. The Exxilons.
12. Earth and Draconia.
13. The Biomorphic Organisational Systems Supervisor, the giant computer which ran Global Chemicals in Llanfairfach and attempted to take over the world.
14. Miss Hawthorne.
15. Underneath Wenley Moor in Derbyshire.
16. An alien mind-parasite used by the Master.
17. For allegedly looting.
18. Sarah's aunt and a prominent virologist.
19. Daemos (60,000 light years away from Earth).
20. By reversing the polarity of the radio telescope.

1. In the battle with the Thals one of the Daleks accidentally destroyed the Dalek City's generators, thus stopping the flow of static electricity on which the Daleks were dependent.
2. Zephon.
3. By the intervention of a fleet of rockets from the planet Hyperon (*see Genesis of the Daleks*).
4. He gave the Thals a chemical formula which weakened the protective dome of the Kaled City, so rendering the city vulnerable to the Thals' rocket.
5. Because the Kaled scientific elite were against his continuing the development of the Daleks.
6. Jenny.
7. To protect them from intruders.
8. He deflected the bomb with a barrier built across the shaft down which it was dropped.
9. Bragen.
10. Marc Cory.
11. With the Doctor's knowledge of future Dalek defeats, Davros could then forewarn his creations of their mistakes.
12. Because each side was fighting the war using computer logic; each move of one side was countered by a perfectly logical move on the other side.
13. If the Aridians did not hand over the Doctor and his companions, then the Daleks would destroy the entire Aridian race.
14. To use the icecanos of Spiridon to put a vast army of Daleks into suspended animation until they were ready to conquer the Galaxy; and also to investigate the Spiridons' invisibility.
15. He was protected by a force-field, and put himself into a form of suspended animation.
16. To help them conquer their Human enemies.
17. By observing Jamie's reactions as he attempted to rescue Victoria.
18. The Doctor sabotaged a mercury fluid link, without

which the TARDIS could not dematerialise. Only in the Dalek City could the TARDIS crew find more mercury.

19. With deadly bacteria.
20. Kristas; Ganatus; Elyon (who died in the Lake of Mutations); Antodus (who fell down a chasm).

1. To escape the vengeance of the Black Guardian of Time.
2. Terradon.
3. The Nimon.
4. Jackson; Herrick; Orfe; Tala.
5. Fang Rock.
6. The Great Vampire.
7. The Kraals.
8. Small, carnivorous, snake-like creatures found on the planet of the Sevateem.
9. It was put into a time loop by the Time Lords to counter the menace of the Fendahl.
10. So that crooked art dealers would believe that the Leonardo 'fakes', which Scaroth planned to sell, were the genuine article. The Louvre painting was destroyed by fire, and the Doctor replaced it with one of the 'fakes'!
11. Meglos.
12. By economic manipulation and extortion.
13. Magnus Greel.
14. The Eye of Horus, the control point of the force field which kept Sutekh imprisoned in Egypt, and which was protected by the Guardians of Horus.
15. Professor Sorenson. The Doctor insisted that he should sacrifice himself by ejecting himself into space so that his fellow Morestrans could leave Zeta Minor.
16. Only the time-sensitive Tharils could navigate the ship through Zero Point.
17. To promote understanding between alien races.
18. She convinced the Daleks she was dead by stopping her hearts and was taken to the surface by other slave workers to be buried.
19. Leader of Skonnos and High Priest of the Nimon.
20. Gallifreyans who rejected the Time Lord way of life and live in the wastelands of Gallifrey.

1. Steven Taylor; Zoe; Sarah Jane Smith; Adric.
2. Adric.
3. They were 'kidnapped' by the Doctor who feared that they might give away the secret of the TARDIS and of his and Susan's presence on Earth if he let them go.
4. Professor Marius.
5. Sara Kingdom.
6. Dido.
7. To help the Tharils in their efforts to abolish slavery in E-Space; and to avoid having to return to Gallifrey in N-Space.
8. Zoe (by Leo Ryan in *The Wheel in Space*).
9. Sarah Jane Smith.
10. Because of her striking resemblance to his grand-daughter, Susan.
11. Leela.
12. By her willingness to sacrifice herself to save the Doctor's life. (Such irrationality so confused Azal that he destroyed himself.)
13. They were sent back by the Time Lords after the Doctor had been tried for his crimes.
14. Susan and Barbara.
15. Victoria's (in *Fury from the Deep*).

1. Vortis.
2. It was originally designed as a justice machine which passed absolutely fair judgements. The Marinians developed it into a computer capable of controlling men's minds and thus eliminated all wars from their planet.
3. The Daleks.
4. Condensation which formed on the inside walls of the TARDIS.
5. In a house of horrors at the Festival of Ghana.
6. Molybdenum.
7. While attempting to absorb the Doctor's life force, he also acquired his conscience and saw the error of his people's ways.
8. Bennett.
9. Their ships had each been disabled in a skirmish in space.
10. Lobos.
11. *The Keys of Marinus.*
12. It was built on stilts above the jungle.
13. Vrestin; Hrostar; Prapillus; Hlynia; Hilio.
14. On the planet Tigus.
15. She had become infected with DN6; if she remained miniaturised the poison would kill her.
16. As a prison world for convicted murderers.
17. Cyril the schoolboy, in the Celestial Toymaker's domain.
18. In the head of the giant Monoid statue on the Ark.
19. Arbitan.
20. Skaro.

1. United Nations Intelligence Taskforce.
2. That he be given laboratory facilities to repair the grounded TARDIS.
3. The Yeti invasion of London.
4. The Old Priory, the home of the Scarman brothers.
5. In London during the Yeti invasion of that city.
6. Harry Sullivan.
7. Geneva.
8. Mike Yates.
9. The Brigadier and Sergeant Benton (in *The Three Doctors*).
10. Mike Yates.
11. He blew up the Silurians' caves, so sealing them off forever.
12. Brigade Leader Lethbridge-Stewart and Security Officer Elizabeth Shaw.
13. Because he drew a gun on the Doctor and the Brigadier due to his involvement in Operation Golden Age.
14. To investigate the destruction of several North Sea oil rigs, caused, as the Doctor discovered, by the Zygons' Skarasen.
15. By using the blue anti-hypnosis crystal he had found on Metebelis Three.

1. The Hostile Action Displacement System, a system whereby, if the TARDIS is attacked, it dematerialises and, shortly afterwards, rematerialises somewhere else.
2. The lama Padmasambhava.
3. Plankton.
4. Ben Jackson.
5. Caven.
6. The Master Brain which controlled the Land of Fiction.
7. Sam (Samantha) Briggs.
8. The Weed Creature.
9. Lady Jennifer Buckingham and Lieutenant Jeremy Carstairs.
10. An island devastated by atomic war on which there was a war museum.
11. To halt the steady advance of the glaciers.
12. Giles Kent.
13. To ask for his assistance in giving the TARDIS a much needed overhaul.
14. Zondal.
15. Because one of the mercury fluid links had been broken.
16. A rocket builder on Earth who helped the Doctor, Jamie and Zoe in their struggle against the Ice Warriors.
17. Space and Inter-time Directional Robot All-purpose Transporter.
18. Because the Doctor was forced to operate the TARDIS's emergency unit to escape volcanic eruptions on the planet Dulkis (in the previous adventure *The Dominators*).
19. Because it was only by absorbing the radioactive energy which Dulkis's destruction would provide that their space fleet could be powered.
20. With sulphuric acid.

1. He hoped to destroy a Viking invasion of the Northumberland coast with atomic bazookas, and thereby ensure that King Harold would be sufficiently fresh and rested to defeat William the Conqueror at Hastings.
2. Autloc.
3. The Admiral de Coligny.
4. Za and Kal.
5. *The Gunfighters*.
6. Li H'sen Chang and the Tong of the Black Scorpion.
7. Ixta.
8. Colin McLaren.
9. They convinced their cavemen captors they were dead by assembling a pile of skulls and burning sticks. The cavemen believed that the time travellers' bodies had been consumed by fire.
10. In the Conciergerie prison in Paris.
11. He claimed that his music was so exquisite that only those sensitive and cultured enough could appreciate it; no one wished to admit that he was lacking in good taste and everyone applauded the Doctor!
12. Delos.
13. He ran a trail of honey from Ian's arm to an ant hill and threatened to let the ants eat him alive.
14. Tegana.
15. The TARDIS.

1. Rassilon.
2. The Minyans' destruction of Minyos. The Time Lords had helped the Minyans to achieve nuclear capability.
3. They surrounded it with a force-field.
4. Omega.
5. It is the energy source which is the foundation of Time Lord civilisation. It is located underneath the Panopticon in the Capitol.
6. Castellan Kelner.
7. Twelve.
8. Because he believed that his fellow Time Lords had abandoned him after he had detonated the star which enabled the Time Lords to travel through time. (In fact the Time Lords thought that he had died in the explosion, and honoured him as one of their greatest heroes.)
9. To prevent their creation; to alter their development so that they would evolve into less aggressive creatures; or to find some inherent weakness in them.
10. For his part in leading an army in an attempt to conquer the Galaxy.
11. The leader of the Prydonian chapter of Time Lords, and a former teacher of the Doctor at the Academy. When the Doctor returned to Gallifrey to stop the Vardan/Sontaran invasion, Borusa was both Chancellor and acting-President of the Time Lords.
12. Because the Time Lords had insufficient power to achieve a full physical manifestation.
13. A huge communal brain, storehouse of all the personality imprints of all Time Lords that have ever lived, which is used by the Time Lords to monitor life in the Capitol and to predict future events.
14. Rassilon.
15. The Master; the Meddling Monk; the War Chief; Omega; Morbius; Chancellor Goth; Castellan Kelner.

1. A 20th-century diplomat and peacemaker. The guerillas wanted to kill him because they believed him to have been responsible for the Third World War which paved the way for a Dalek take-over of Earth.
2. With a deadly virus.
3. To penetrate the Earth's crust and tap pockets of Stahlmann's gas, a vast new source of energy.
4. It had been totally destroyed by the corroding effect of the light beam.
5. By the introduction of a piece of positive matter (the second Doctor's recorder) into Omega's world of anti-matter.
6. Because his home planet, which was rapidly running out of natural resources, wished to make a separate and independent treaty with Peladon, by which it would benefit from its mineral wealth.
7. Humans.
8. A dragon-like omnivore which lives in swamps. A small herd of the creatures was imprisoned in Vorg's Scope.
9. Linx the Sontaran.
10. To the Doctor, and, when he refused, to the Master.
11. Because of overcrowding on Earth.
12. King Peladon's Chancellor who was killed by Aggedor.
13. By heat.
14. During a space plague, which he cured – and was therefore created a noble of Draconia.
15. A Solonian chief whom the Doctor helped to achieve successful mutation into a god-like super-being.
16. Commander Azaxyr.
17. Because of his knowledge of time travel, which would enable them to ransack planets throughout time.
18. Professor Cliff Jones. A fungus which Jones had developed to solve the world's food shortage.
19. Arak and Tuar.
20. The blue crystal was the one missing link in a giant web which would expand the Great One's mind to infinity and, so she thought, give her absolute power.

1. The Cybermen.
2. With the help of a fungus growth which absorbed Earth's oxygen, so turning Earth into a planet more suitable for the Ice Warriors.
3. The Doctor planned to drain the mind of the Great Intelligence. The plan failed when his friends, believing the Intelligence to be draining *his* mind, 'rescued' him.
4. Because the radiation levels on their own planet were becoming more and more intolerable.
5. To take over the best brains in the country – including the Doctor's.
6. They would suffocate people by spraying an almost invisible plastic film over their faces.
7. They intended to melt the polar ice caps, raise the planet's temperature and construct lakes in which to breed herds of Skarasen.
8. To demonstrate Broton's strength to the delegates at an international energy conference.
9. Sergeant Arnold.
10. General Carrington.
11. To clear Central London of undesirable elements, prior to their rolling time back to a Golden Age.
12. Towards the end of the 20th century.
13. By a reprogrammed War Machine.
14. To drain Earth's energy.
15. By acting as a go-between in negotiations between the two races.

1. At the Pharos Project on Earth.
2. He received a telepathic warning from the Matrix.
3. A form of alien plant-life which feeds on animal life.
4. Styggron. He died when he became infected with the deadly virus he himself had developed.
5. The remains of Erato's spaceship.
6. Commander Sharrel.
7. To prevent anyone stealing their Elixir of Life.
8. The Doctor blew the economy apart by introducing a 2 per cent growth tax, index-linked, into the Company's computer.
9. Commander Uvanov; and Dask (in reality, Taren Capel); Toos; Zilda; Poul; Cass; Chub; Borg; Kerril.
10. Professor Marcus Scarman.
11. The Savants are the scientifically minded half of Tigellan society, the Deons the religious half.
12. They destroyed their own race bank, and in so doing brought to an end the entire Kastrian race.
13. For daring to blaspheme against Xoanon.
14. An ancient Chinese god, and the identity assumed by the war criminal Magnus Greel in 19th-century China and London.
15. The Loch Ness Monster, half-animal, half-machine, created by the Zygons.
16. By absorbing the energy from the Disintegrator Gun, which the Brigadier used in an attempt to destroy it.
17. The then Keeper of Traken.
18. Mena.
19. The Anti-Matter Monster.
20. A Rutan scout.

1. The TARDIS. (This was our very first sight of the TARDIS.)
2. Jamie, in *The Wheel in Space*.
3. The Seeds of Death were the seeds sent by the Ice Warriors to Earth to change the atmosphere, ready for the Martians' colonisation of the planet. The Seeds of Doom were the two Krynoid pods found in the Antarctic.
4. A horse box (*Terror of the Autons*); a small spaceship (*Colony in Space*); a computer bank (*The Time Monster*); a grandfather clock (*The Deadly Assassin* and *The Keeper of Traken*); a stone pillar (*Logopolis*); a police box (*Logopolis*).
5. The Daleks and the Thals.
6. A Type Forty.
7. *The Ark*.
8. Not to harm Humans.
9. A Dalek (it is the travel machine in which the mutated Dalek form travels).
10. In his first incarnation, while fighting the Dalek Master Plan. He met both the Daleks and the Meddling Monk there.
11. The Daleks; the War Lords, aided by the War Chief; the Guardians of Time; the Tharils; the Chronovores.
12. Because the Doctor allows them to share a telepathic Time Lord gift.
13. Beneath the control console.
14. That of K'anpo Rimpoche (Cho-je).
15. The Kraals – Oseidon; the Visians – Mira; the Marsh Spiders – Alzarius; Aggedor – Peladon; the Ice Warriors – Mars; Sutekh – Phaester Osiris; the Mutants – Solos; the Optera – Vortis.

1. (i) A lump of the mineral Jethryk; (ii) the planet Calufrax; (iii) the Great Seal of Diplos (Vivien Fay's pendant); (iv) part of a statue belonging to the Gracht family of Tara; (v) a holy relic of the Swampies on Delta Three; (vi) Princess Astra of Atrios.
2. The White Guardian of Time.
3. To enable the White Guardian to restore the natural balance of good and evil in the Universe and prevent it from slipping into eternal chaos.
4. The core of the Key to Time. It could also be used to locate the various segments of the Key, and to transform them into their proper forms.
5. Cyrrhenis Minima (it was then taken by Garron to Ribos).
6. So he could use Ribos as a base to help him regain the throne of Levithia.
7. He saw the possibility of employing a vast army of mercenaries to help him take the Levithian throne.
8. The Shrivenzales.
9. Unstoffe.
10. Because he believed that Ribos revolved around its sun, and that the stars in the sky were not ice crystals but individual suns, each with its own system of planets.
11. Zanak, an empty shell of a planet which materialised around smaller planets and plundered them for their valuable minerals.
12. *Vantarialis.*
13. She needed the energy produced to power the time dams which kept her body in suspended animation.
14. Psychic energy was released every time Zanak ransacked another planet.
15. The number of stones in the circle varied, there being at times six, seven or nine stones. Three of these were Ogri; after the destruction of two Ogri and the deportation of a third, Cessair of Diplos was transformed by the Megara into a stone, fixing the total of the stones at seven.

16. The archaelogist who helped the Doctor, Romana and K9 to defeat Cessair.
17. For removing the Great Seals which kept the Megara in isolation on the spaceship bound for Diplos.
18. With murder and the removal and misuse of the Great Seal of Diplos (in reality, the third segment of the Key to Time).
19. Vivien Fay.
20. Ogros, in the Tau Ceti system.

1. When Yartek, the leader of the Voords, inserted a fake key into the machine and it blew up.
2. He sought out Charles Preslin, the germinologist.
3. By climbing down a 1,500-foot-long cable from the roof of the City.
4. Susan.
5. The Crater of Needles.
6. The Mire Beasts.
7. He supplied their spaceship with power from the TARDIS.
8. Because she believed that it intended to harm Vicki.
9. By draining the life force of the Savages.
10. To link up with other computers and become a sort of universal problem-solver.
11. Ian.
12. Whipsnade Zoo!
13. With the Menoptera's cell destructor.
14. The Sensorites.
15. He was disgusted at the Doctor's apparently callous disregard for the life of Anne Chaplette, the French girl they left behind in the St Bartholomew's Day Massacre. The Doctor did not dare take her with them because of the danger of rewriting history.

1. Because they needed his help to defeat their Movellan enemies.
2. By threatening to take Dyoni, Alydon's fiancée, to the Daleks, he succeeded in making the Thals realise that there were some things about which they cared enough to fight.
3. The readiness to obey, fight, destroy and exterminate.
4. The Time Destructor.
5. Ian Chesterton.
6. Dortmun.
7. He was put into cryogenic suspension and taken by Tyssan to Earth to stand trial for his crimes against Humanity.
8. Earth.
9. Bettan.
10. Taranium. On Uranus.
11. Theodore Maxtible.
12. Nyder.
13. To investigate the use of time travel equipment in that century, and to ensure that all the diplomats assembled at the house of Sir Reginald Styles were killed, so paving the way for a Dalek invasion of Earth.
14. Taron; Rebec; Latep; Marat; Vaber; Codal.
15. Dan Galloway.
16. By overloading their power source.
17. A small case of anti-radiation drugs.
18. Vicki.
19. That he should take the Dalek Factor and spread it throughout the entire history of Earth.
20. Temmosus.

1. At Luigi Rossini's circus.
2. Mr Magister, the Vicar of Devil's End; Colonel Masters; Professor Keller; Professor Thascales; a Special Commissioner from Sirius Four.
3. He planned to provoke a world war in which he would emerge the only victor.
4. TOMTIT (Transmission Of Matter Through Interstitial Time).
5. To use the power sealed in the Eye of Harmony to renew his regeneration cycle, and in so doing also have his final revenge on the Time Lords by destroying Gallifrey.
6. Colonel George Trenchard.
7. By the use of a hypnotic device which convinced Earthmen that Draconians were attacking their space-ships and vice-versa.
8. To help them to awaken the rest of their kindred throughout the world.
9. By taking over the body of Tremas, Nyssa's father.
10. Faced with arrest by the Atlantean palace guards, he called down upon Atlantis the wrath of Kronos.
11. Traken was destroyed as a consequence of the Master's interference with the Logopolitan Program, which preserved the Universe beyond its point of natural heat-death.
12. To hold the peoples of the Universe to ransom by threatening to destroy them with the Doomsday Machine if they did not submit themselves to his rule.
13. Because the Doctor pleaded for his freedom.
14. On Traken.
15. By threatening to close the CVE, on which the life of the Universe depended, if the Universe did not accept continued existence under his 'guidance'.

1. Because of his interference in the affairs of others; and for stealing a TARDIS.
2. They believed they were attacking the missile silos of war-mongers. Salamander persuaded them to remain underground by telling them that surface radioactivity made it unwise for them to leave their underground base.
3. Because the beacons were made of argonite, a valuable mineral.
4. Atlanteans who could live underwater and who were used to gather the foodstocks of plankton. Polly was almost turned into one.
5. In Tibet, forty years previously.
6. On natural gas from the North Sea.
7. It was originally a teaching machine.
8. Clent.
9. To use his knowledge to conquer Earth.
10. An Atlantean surgeon who became leader of the survivors of Atlantis after the defeat of the mad Professor Zaroff.
11. Khrisong.
12. Ta.
13. He planned to drain the ocean into the Earth's core, so causing the super-heated steam to blow the planet in two.
14. Selris.
15. To operate the drive mechanism of their Dynotrope.

1. The Prydonian chapter.
2. A secret Time Lord agency which occasionally interferes in the affairs of the Universe when such action is deemed to be absolutely necessary.
3. The Minyans.
4. A record of information, including an account of the defeat of the Giant Vampires, which was installed in all Type Forty TARDISes.
5. As an aid to bodily regeneration.
6. The De-mat gun.
7. In gratitude for defeating Omega, thereby saving Gallifrey.
8. It remained in the possession of the Chancellor of the Time Lords.
9. It created a supernova, so providing Gallifrey with a new energy source.
10. Chancellor Goth.
11. That history should not be distorted and that no individual should be allowed to cross his own time stream. This law was broken when the Time Lords brought together the first, second and third Doctors to combat the Omega menace.
12. She was a member of Gallifrey's space traffic control, responsible for monitoring all traffic movement around Gallifrey.
13. The Meddling Monk.
14. With their bowships.
15. He ensured that, while the Sash and the Rod were in the possession of the President, only the Chancellor of the Time Lords knew the location of the Great Key.

1. He intended to use the Cybermen in his Brotherhood of Logicians' attempt to gain power.
2. Because of the severe consequences it might have for Earth. The Doctor preferred to wait until Mondas destroyed itself.
3. He loaded a Cybermat with gold dust and attacked the Cybermen with it. (Gold is deadly to Cybermen.)
4. Hobson.
5. They used Cybermats which carried a deadly venom.
6. Toberman, Kaftan's manservant.
7. They took Polly as a hostage.
8. Because of the danger of radiation.
9. She realised that the Cybermen could be destroyed by spraying their chest units with a mixture of solvents.
10. They loaded Space Beacon Nerva with cobalt bombs and set it on a collision course to Voga.
11. *The Tomb of the Cybermen*.
12. He developed depolarisers which, when taped to the back of the neck, jammed the Cyber control waves.
13. By the Gravitron, which neutralised their gravity and sent them flying off into space.
14. Kellman.
15. Professor Parry. Eric Klieg and Kaftan.
16. To use it as a base from which to launch the Cyber fleet that was to invade Earth.
17. With the Skystriker rocket.
18. By poisoning the Moonbase's sugar supplies.
19. Because their power source was destroyed in the disintegration of Mondas.
20. Because of its great mineral wealth.

1. Alien ambassadors to Earth, who were first encountered by General Carrington.
2. They were rich in trisilicate, a mineral essential to the war effort.
3. An incarnation of K'anpo, the Doctor's hermit mentor.
4. For Ky, a Solonian chief. It contained tablets which led the Doctor to the discovery that the mutation of the Solonians was part of a natural process.
5. By spreading fear and panic among the miners through the use of a hologram of Aggedor, the royal beast of Peladon.
6. Azal the Daemon and his spaceship.
7. Bellal.
8. They came to the 20th century to kill Styles, who they believed had murdered delegates to a World Peace Conference. In reality, it was the guerillas themselves who had caused the fatal explosion in their efforts to kill Styles.
9. An Earth scientist who found refuge from the Marshal in the thaesium mines on Solos, where he continued his research and lived with the Mutants.
10. He planned to release the Drashigs from Vorg's Miniscope. Since Vorg and the Scope were only on Inter Minor by Zarb's permission, the President would be blamed for the ensuing devastation.
11. Florana.
12. John Ashe.
13. Stubbs and Cotton.
14. Vega Nexos.
15. As a result of the psychic experiments of Lupton and his colleagues.
16. The head of the IMC operations on the planet of the Doomsday Machine, Exarius.
17. Wester.
18. The Silurians and the Sea Devils.
19. A huge shapeless monster which feeds on the Ogrons.
20. Because all the cells of his body had been devastated by the crystals on Metebelis Three.

1. Catherine de Medici.
2. So that, by 1979, Mankind would have reached a sufficiently high level of technological achievement to be able to construct the time machine which Scaroth needed to travel 400 million years back in time to prevent the extinction of the Jagaroth.
3. Kublai Khan.
4. Hieronymous.
5. By the marriage of his sister, Joanna, to Saphadin, the brother of Saladin.
6. Aeneas.
7. The terrified crew deserted their ship when the Daleks, whom they believed to be the White Barbary Terror, appeared on board in pursuit of the Doctor and his companions.
8. Because she was against Human sacrifices. She also threatened the High Priest's authority among the Aztecs.
9. They regularly heard the chanting of a brotherhood of monks, which was, in reality, a recording.
10. Susan, in *The Aztecs*.
11. To assassinate the Emperor Nero.
12. Diomede.
13. They wanted him to turn the Doctor, whom they believed to be Doc Holliday, over to them.
14. To take his prisoners into slavery in the West Indies.
15. He accidentally set fire, with his spectacle lens, to Nero's rejected plans for a perfect city.

1. Meglos.
2. He became insane when the Doctor attempted to repair him using a direct mind-to-computer link and forgot to erase his own personality from the computer.
3. It was a device which imprisoned living samples of a planet's flora and fauna on laser crystals. It started to malfunction when the *Empress* and the *Hecate* crashed into each other as they were leaving hyper-space and the matter interfaces were rendered unstable.
4: It was originally a space beacon.
5. *Image of the Fendahl.*
6. To establish a trading treaty between Chloris and his home world of Tythonus.
7. Madame Nostradamus.
8. The Deciders.
9. Aneth.
10. He needed the Doctor's head to house the brain of Morbius.
11. A Krynoid pod (a second pod was later discovered by the Doctor).
12. The Company who put a series of six miniature suns in orbit around Pluto.
13. Because of solar flares.
14. The ship computer of the *P7E* which developed megalomaniac tendencies and ruled the planet which formed around the *P7E.*
15. Dwarf star alloy. It was the only substance which could hold the Tharils in captivity.
16. Salyavin, a retired Time Lord.
17. He pierced it through the heart, using a spaceship as a stake.
18. They experienced a disruption in the time field.
19. Otherwise known as Dask, he was the madman who organised the robots' revolt on the Sandminer.
20. In the body of Dune, one of the Ark's technicians, who was lying in a state of cryogenic preservation.

1. Princess Strella.
2. The peasants.
3. He imprisoned the rightful heir to the Taran throne, Prince Reynart, in his castle, so ensuring that the Prince would forego his right to the crown by being absent from the coronation. This plan was foiled when the Doctor repaired an android double of Reynart, which was crowned in his place.
4. The surgeon and former lover of Count Grendel.
5. Androids were needed to replace the nine-tenths of their population who had died in a plague.
6. He planned to make Romana Queen by marrying her to Reynart; he then intended to kill Reynart, marry Romana himself, and, by Taran laws of succession, become King of Tara.
7. By swallowing the fifth segment of the Key to Time.
8. To refine protein from the methane on Delta Three.
9. They had been sent to Delta Three when Earthmen colonised Delta Magna.
10. A pressure group on Delta Magna which wanted the Refinery closed down and the Swampies to be left in peace. Dugeen belonged to this group.
11. The machinery of the Refinery on Delta Three.
12. By detecting surface vibrations.
13. Thawn, the head of the Refinery on Delta Three, as an excuse to exterminate the Swampies, and to compromise the Sons of Earth.
14. The Shadow.
15. Atrios.
16. Drax, a Time Lord.
17. A program built into the computer Mentalis. Under attack from the Marshal, it was programmed to destroy both Atrios and Zeos, so ensuring that neither side would win the war.
18. The Marshal.
19. To prevent Mentalis approaching zero on its countdown, and to stop the Marshal attacking Zeos. He

managed to do this by using the Key to Time (or, more precisely, five segments of the Key and a makeshift sixth segment made of chronodyne).

20. By impersonating the White Guardian and asking to be given the Key for safe-keeping.

1. To gain mastery over all time and space.
2. In return for shelter, Linx promised to supply Irongron with technologically advanced weapons, including guns and a robot knight.
3. The probic vent, at the back of the neck.
4. To use Earth as a strategic base in their war with the Sontarans.
5. Hal the archer.
6. He needed their skills and equipment to help him repair his crippled spaceship.
7. The Vardans.
8. To exhaust the Sontaran (who was unused to Earth's gravity). Styre would then have to return to his ship to recharge himself with his Energiser, which Harry had sabotaged.
9. He uses it to recharge himself with energy.
10. That of Reuben, the lighthouse keeper at Fang Rock.
11. Stor.
12. To use it as a base for their conquest of the Galaxy.
13. Ruta Three.
14. By enveloping the island with a thick fog.
15. With a crude laser beam.

1. They fed on its milk.
2. By RAF bombers.
3. To the Sevateem, the Doctor, whose 'Face of Evil' was carved into a mountain, was the Evil One who they believed kept their god, Xoanon, in captivity. To the Tesh, he was the Lord of Time, whose coming to save them had been foretold.
4. It was a research hospital in the Asteroid Belt, to which Leela took the Doctor when he was infected by the Virus Nucleus.
5. The samples would have provided a vast new source of energy for Morestra. They were unable to leave with the samples because the Anti-Matter creatures on Zeta Minor would not allow them to do so, and dragged their ship back down to the planet's surface until every last sample of anti-matter had been returned.
6. That he would help them in the establishment of the second Skonnan Empire.
7. To have his TARDIS's chameleon circuit repaired.
8. Varsh, the brother of Adric.
9. The Fendahl is the monstrous creature from the fifth planet which feeds on life itself. It is composed of twelve Fendahleen, large snake-like creatures against which salt is the only defence. The Fendahl Core is the medium through which the Fendahl manifests itself. When the Doctor and Leela fought the emergent Fendahl on Earth, the scientist Thea Ransome had become the Fendahl Core.
10. Noah. He was succeeded by Vira.
11. It takes two minutes for radio waves to travel from Mars (where the Eye of Horus was located) to Earth (where Sutekh was imprisoned).
12. By promising one day to restore to him his missing arm (which, unknown to Condo, had been used as part of the Morbius monster).
13. Mandrel.
14. Tigella.

15. The henchwoman of Lady Adrasta of Chloris.
16. The *P7E*.
17. When killed by a massive dose of heat, they break down into vraxoin, the most dangerous addictive drug in the Universe.
18. Duggan.
19. Poul and the robot D84. They were there because of written threats from Taren Capel of robot rebellion.
20. The spaceship *Hydrax*.

1. Cambridge.
2. Katarina.
3. Peladon.
4. David Campbell.
5. The Elders and the Savages.
6. Ian Chesterton.
7. Polly and Ben.
8. Leela.
9. Harry Sullivan.
10. To look after Leela,
11. He had to return to Gallifrey and was unable to take Sarah with him.
12. They used the Daleks' time machine which they found deserted on Mechanus.
13. It was only by remaining on the other side of the mirror that he could survive the damage he had sustained from the time winds.
14. Tegan.
15. Jamie, Zoe, Leela, K9 (Mark One) and, presumably, Susan.

1. He insisted that there would only be peace in the Universe when the Daleks had conquered all other life forms.
2. To guarantee her father's co-operation.
3. They hoped that the Daleks would provide them with food and would be willing to join with them in an attempt to rebuild Skaro.
4. An anti-Dalek device, programmed to explode whenever a Dalek approached.
5. By holding Sara and Steven as hostages.
6. A Kaled scientist and member of the scientific elite who was dissatisfied with the way Davros's experiments were progressing.
7. By promising to give him the secret of turning base metal into gold.
8. In Bedfordshire.
9. With the directional unit he 'borrowed' from the Meddling Monk's TARDIS.
10. The Doctor. Because he unwittingly passed an intelligence test which proved him a suitable subject for robotisation.
11. By blowing up the Incubator Room on Skaro, he was able to set the Daleks' development back by about a thousand years.
12. By unleashing the fury of an icecano which refroze the Dalek army into suspended animation.
13. The process was designed only to turn Humans into Daleks; the Doctor survived because he is not Human.
14. The Master.
15. By using the Daleks' own Time Destructor.

1. The mysterious power source of Tigella, which was coveted by Meglos.
2. By absorbing the life forces of young women.
3. Crinoth.
4. By sending him down a space time tunnel until he finally died.
5. They had put a series of six miniature suns in orbit around the planet.
6. Guy Crayford.
7. By killing the guests, many of whom were important men of learning (including Leonardo da Vinci), Mandragora intended to check Earth's progress and so eliminate the possibility of Earth's one day becoming a galactic power strong enough to pose a threat to Mandragora.
8. Leela.
9. They had heard no news from Erato, their ambassador to Chloris, and so, fearing the worst, they aimed a neutron star at Chloris's sun.
10. Nesbin.
11. As Zanak tried to materialise around Earth, the Doctor and Romana materialised the TARDIS in exactly the same point in space and time.
12. Pangol.
13. By announcing his candidacy for the office of President of the Time Lords.
14. The Monitor.
15. The Swarm's incubation chambers on Titan were blown up by the Doctor. (The idea was Leela's although the Doctor later claimed it was his!)
16. He released helium into the air, so changing Taren Capel's voice, and a robot (SV7), unable to recognise its master's voice, killed him.
17. Idas.
18. The *Empress* and the *Hecate*.
19. They were all different stages in the Alzarian line of evolution.
20. Because his body was shattered when he fell from the tower of the Pharos Project on Earth.

1. (a) The Meddling Monk. (b) The interim stage between the Doctor's fourth and fifth regenerations.
2. The TARDIS key is coded to the Doctor's own molecular structure and can only be used by him; if someone else needs to use the key, the Doctor must make a telepathic adjustment to the key. (The TARDIS has a trimonic locking system, opened by a cypher-indent key; the lock has twenty-one positions, only one of which can open the door – any other position would cause the lock to melt.)
3. One of the third Doctor's cars: it was a futuristic vehicle which resembled a flying saucer and could indeed fly.
4. The Daleks. All the rest are robots.
5. Skaro, the planet of the Daleks.
6. A black-ended gold rod which controls the temporal drive of the TARDIS. Once it is removed, the interior of the Doctor's TARDIS becomes that of an ordinary police box. It was removed in *The Wheel In Space* when mercury vapour from the TARDIS's broken fluid links threatened to poison the Doctor and Jamie.
7. The Ice Lords and the Ice Warriors.
8. The robot created by Professor Kettlewell to help in his misguided attempts to create a better world. It was accidentally turned into a giant robot by the Brigadier.
9. Mars.
10. Robot deactivation discs, small discs used to mark robots which have been deactivated.
11. Because the TARDIS control room rests in a state of temporal grace.
12. The prison world of the Time Lords.
13. It was destroyed by the Fendahl on its way to Earth. The Company made Mars habitable again. (These facts seem to contradict the history of the Ice Warriors.)
14. Two forms of instantaneous transportation. T-Mat was used on Earth in the 21st century; Trans-mat was used much later between Space Station Nerva and Earth.
15. Because they are all dimensionally transcendental – the inside and the outside exist in different dimensions.

1. On television: William Hartnell; Patrick Troughton; Jon Pertwee; Tom Baker; Peter Davison (Edmund Warwick often stood in for William Hartnell, and stuntman Terry Walsh for Jon Pertwee). On film: Peter Cushing. On stage: Trevor Martin.
2. Anthony Coburn.
3. The role of Bret Vyon, the Space Security agent and brother of Sara Kingdom.
4. On Saturday, 23 November 1963 (at 5.15 pm).
5. Ron Grainer.
6. Barbara Wright, one of the Doctor's first companions.
7. Terry Nation.
8. *Logopolis* (he appeared in the last few seconds of the final episode).
9. Roger Delgado; Peter Pratt; Geoffrey Beevers; Anthony Ainley.
10. Terrance Dicks.
11. A 1974 *Doctor Who* stage play, written by Terrance Dicks, and starring Trevor Martin as the Doctor and Wendy Padbury (who played Zoe in the television series) as Jenny, one of his assistants.
12. Douglas Adams, the writer of *The Hitch-hiker's Guide to the Galaxy*.
13. Jean Marsh (who played the role of Sara Kingdom).
14. Verity Lambert.
15. John Leeson and David Brierley.
16. John Cleese and Eleanor Bron (in *City of Death*).
17. Ian Marter (who played the role of Harry Sullivan).
18. Havoc.
19. Peter Davison – he played the part of Tristan in *All Creatures Great and Small*.
20. Caroline John – Liz Shaw; Lalla Ward – Romana; Anneke Wills – Polly; Adrienne Hill – Katarina; Louise Jameson – Leela; Jackie Lane – Dodo; Maureen O'Brien – Vicki; Wendy Padbury – Zoe.